Mount Sacred

Jon Mathieu

MOUNT SACRED

A BRIEF GLOBAL HISTORY OF HOLY MOUNTAINS SINCE 1500

Copyright © Jon Mathieu

Originally published in German as *Mount Sacred. Eine kurze Globalgeschichte der heiligen Berge seit 1500* (Vienna: Böhlau 2023)

English translation published 2023 by
The White Horse Press, The Old Vicarage, Main Street, Winwick, Cambridgeshire PE28 5PN, UK

Set in 11 point Adobe Garamond Pro

OPEN ACCESS. Text CC BY-NC-ND (reuse of illustrations may not be permitted)
doi: 10.3197/63817505877903.book

British Library Cataloguing in Publication Data
A catalogue record for this book is available from the British Library

ISBN: 978-1-912186-71-6 (PB); 978-1-912186-72-3 (Open Access E-book)

CONTENTS

List of Figures vii
Foreword 1
   Mount Sacred – A Travel Programme 2
   Historical Evidence and Historical Context 3
   How this Book Came About 5

A START IN TWO STAGES

1. How Does a Sacred Mountain Come into Being? 9
   Canonisation in European Terms 9
   Tibetan Mountain Rituals 12
   Arbitrary Sacredness? 16
   The Desert Fathers 19
   Revolutionary Symbolism 20

2. A World between Faith and Knowledge 24
   Chinese Mountain Systematics 25
   Sacred Science in Europe 28
   Mountain Research and Alpinism 32
   From Theology to Religious Studies 35

MOUNTAIN ITINERARIES

3. Mount Kailash – Model Mountain of Holiness 41
   A Global Career 41
   Tantra, Demchock and Shiva 45
   Buddhism for All 47

Contents

4. Tai Shan – The Imperial Eastern Mountain 50
   Landscape as a History Book *51*
   The Rise of the Goddess *53*
   From Revolution to World Heritage Site................. *55*

5. Paektusan – Sacred Mountain of the Revolution............... 58
   The Ancestors of the Manchus *59*
   Korea's Progenitor *61*
   Sacred Revolution in North Korea *62*
   Religious Mountain Worship in Asia *65*

6. Rise of the Christian Crosses.............................. 67
   Iconoclastic Controversies *68*
   The Summits Are Being Christianised *70*
   In the Crossfire of Criticism.......................... *73*

7. The Redeemer in the Italian Mountains 77
   An Idea for the Jubilee Year 1900 .... *78*
   Cristo Redentore *and the Holy Book of Nature* *81*

8. Six Grandfathers and other American Mountains.............. 84
   Superhuman Presidents on Mount Rushmore *85*
   Religious Freedom for Indians? *87*
   Controversial Spirituality in National Parks........... *89*

9. Volcanoes on the East African Rift Valley 92
   Searching for Clues on Mount Kilimanjaro *93*
   A Mountain of God by Hearsay *95*

10. An Inselberg in the Australian Desert..................... 98
   'Stone Age' and 'Dreamtime' *99*
   From Ayers Rock to Uluru *101*
   The Administration of the Sacred *103*

List of Figures

THE JOURNEY CONTINUES

11. What Future for Sacred Mountains? 109
    Religion and Environment, Globally 110
    Colonialism, Anti-Colonialism, 'Nature and Culture' 112
    Social Roles 114
    Environmental and Climate Protection 117
    Mount Sacred – The Twenty-first Century. 119

Select Bibliography 121

Notes 125

Index 149

LIST OF FIGURES

1. Tibetan scroll painting of the Pure Crystal Mountain as a shrine with pilgrims. Courtesy of Heinz J. Zumbühl. 15

2. Hill raised on the Champ de Mars in Paris to worship the Supreme Being. Coloured engraving, 1794. Bibliothèque nationale de France. 22

3. 'Image of the true form of the five peaks', China c. 1614, from Edouard Chavannes, *Le T'ai Chan. Essai de monographie d'un culte chinois* (Paris, 1910). 27

4. Graphic explanations of the theory of the origin of the mountains, from Johann Georg Sulzer, *Johann Jacob Scheuchzers Natur-Geschichten des Schweitzerlandes, samt seinen Reisen über die Schweitzerische Gebürge* (Zurich, 1746). 31

5. The holy Kailash behind Lake Manasarovar on the cover of Sven Hedin's *Transhimalaja: Entdeckungen und Abenteuer in Tibet*, Bd. 3 (Leipzig, 1912). 43

6. Rock inscriptions on the summit of Tai Shan, 2007. Photo: Rolf Müller, Wikimedia Commons, licenced under CC BY-SA 3.0: https://commons.wikimedia.org/wiki/File:Mount_tai_rock_inscriptions.jpg 52

List of Figures

7. Inauguration of the Holy Cross on the Erzberg in 1823. Courtesy of Stadtmuseum Eisenerz, Austria (Tendler-Nachlass). 71

8. 'Cross in the Mountains' by Caspar David Friedrich, 1808. bpk / Staatliche Kunstsammlungen Dresden / Elke Estel / Hans-Peter Klut. 74

9. Map of the summit crosses planned in honour of Christ the Redeemer in Italy, 1899. Courtesy Oscar Gaspari and Gerardo De Meo. 80

10. The Crazy Horse Memorial in the Black Hills, in Custer County, South Dakota, United States (2020). Photo: Jonathunder, Wikimedia Commons, licenced under GNU Free Documentation Licence, Version 1.2; https://en.wikipedia.org/wiki/Crazy_Horse_Memorial#/media/File:CrazyHorse.jpg 87

11. Uluru or Ayers Rock in Central Australia in the first photograph, 1894. Photo: Baldwin Spencer, Victoria Museum, Melbourne, Australia. . 99

FOREWORD

Travelling Gods is the name given to the religious masks in the Indian state of Himachal Pradesh, which are carried on richly decorated palanquins over the steep mountain terrain. Today, they can also make the journey on constructed roads and in motor vehicles. Most villages have such deities. Their journeys lead to other villages or to central places and occasions, for example when the goddess of the former ruling house is deemed to wants to gather her entourage around her. This convocation can also be obviously political. In February 2006, for example, a regional assembly of gods was convened, the likes of which had not been seen for decades. The former *Raja* (ruler) of the Kullu Valley in the Pre-Himalayas was unhappy about a huge tourism project that an American company was proposing to realise in his area. The mountain deities were asked to give their opinion. They did so with the help of selected mediums who fell into a trance and stammered out the oracles' words. The message was clear. 'Divine intervention: No! Gods shoot down ski village project', ran the headline in the *Hindustan Times*.[1] Shortly afterwards, the already-approved project was put on hold by the state.

As chance would have it, I had come to Kullu Valley not long before with an Indian historian friend and two European colleagues. The village at the far end of the valley lies at an altitude of 2,000 metres. There are some 6,000-metre peaks in the surrounding area, but the eight-thousanders are further in the north and west of the huge mountain range. We had not done much 'homework' before this journey. When we arrived at the head of the valley, we saw a large crowd converging on a meadow. A stage had been set up in front, and religious speeches and clanging ritual music sounded from loudspeakers. Our Indian host happily announced an unexpected sight, namely a selection of travelling gods. All we had to do was take off our shoes and push our way through the assembled devotees to a low barrier where the statues were displayed together. We were quite excited; it was a special moment.

The experience, of course, also went beyond my horizons and raised perplexing questions. Without decorated palanquins, the little idols looked rather unspectacular. Did they constitute an unmistakable sign that the mountains of the valley were sacred? Wasn't it a bit more complicated than that? What was the purpose of their mobility if they represented the spiritual power of localities? The travelling deities of Himachal Pradesh continued to fascinate me and were one of the reasons why I later embarked on a research journey that also led through many libraries and finally to this book.

Mount Sacred – A Travel Programme

Mount Sacred, which I have chosen as the short title for the book, does not appear on any map, to my knowledge. It is invented and stands as a cipher for numerous mountains around the globe to which sacredness has been attributed in the past or is attributed in the present. This sacredness is of very varied kinds, but it is different from other, non-religious ways of perceiving mountains. Its relationship to contradictory cultural and political circumstances makes it particularly interesting from a historical point of view. In a sense, the sacred mountains can be used as probes to look behind the exterior of a society. This illuminates both people as part of nature and nature as part of people.[2]

The main part of the book consists of 'site visits' to selected sacred mountains. The presentation is intended to go beyond a brief inventory and to vividly illustrate historical practices and changes. The first three visits are in Asia: Mount Kailash in western Tibet, Tai Shan in the Chinese heartland, Paektusan between Chinese Manchuria and North Korea. We will also have to discuss whether this selection is justified: was and is there a massification of easily graspable mountain holiness in Asia, and how is it to be understood? In the west of the Eurasian landmass, at any rate, we encounter different conditions. For a long time, Christianity wanted little or nothing to do with sacred mountains. Two chapters deal with this peculiar reticence and how it changed over time through the example of the summit crosses. Afterwards, our path leads to the New World, with its clash between European settlers and Native Americans. At Mount Rushmore in South Dakota, for example, four well-known white US presidents stand opposite six lesser-known Native American grandfathers. Finally, prominent mountains in Africa and Australia exemplify the different (post-)colonial and touristic development of cult sites in the global South.

The itinerary covers most continents. The mountains I selected have some historical significance for their areas and illustrate certain framework conditions. It is clear that the selection has a strong subjective bias. It could have been done differently, for example by including a mountain from Islamic regions (but I suspect that this would not have changed the main result of the study very much).[3] Before and after the mountain itineraries and site visits, I discuss general questions around Mount Sacred, especially how one can imagine or *not* imagine the emergence of sacred mountains and what future they might

Historical Evidence and Historical Context

have. More generally, this study is about human–environment relations under different cultural conditions, and what we can learn from them. This touches on many issues that are currently much discussed: colonialism, anti-colonialism and indigeneity, gender, tourism, environmental and climate protection, to name only the most important.

Historically, the present study is mainly limited to the post-medieval 'modern' period since 1500. Depending on the topic, either the early modern era is sparsely documented, or important sources start already in the Middle Ages. A pragmatic approach is recommended here. But antiquity is only up for discussion if its traditions live into modern times. Olympus was undoubtedly a mountain of the gods in ancient Greece: was it still so in the sixteenth to twenty-first centuries? The same applies to the biblical tradition. Especially in the Old Testament, there are a number of significant passages about mountains: how were these used in modern times?

The period around 1500 is considered the beginning of Europe's commercial and colonialist expansion, which led to worldwide imperialism in the nineteenth century. The exchange between the continents also influenced religious conditions and the way mountains were treated. The Western contribution to a new 'global' mountain culture was not of a Christian-religious nature, but consisted primarily of the alpinist conquest of summit regions. Around 1900, mountaineering clubs already existed in numerous places, from New Zealand, Asia and Africa, to the United States of America.[4] The strongest religious impulses for mountain culture, on the other hand, came from Tibetan Buddhism, whose symbols have become widely accepted since the late twentieth century. Tibetan prayer flags can be seen today at mountain huts in most Western countries. Sometimes the symbolism is given a certain push, as in 2005, when a group of Italian alpinists erected a statue of the Buddha instead of a summit cross on a difficult mountain, which caused quite a stir.[5] As a rule, however, the religious allusions are mixed with a modern attitude to life that is attracted to spirituality, esotericism and 'places of power'.

Historical Evidence and Historical Context

Historically, the sanctity of mountains can be grasped, among other things, by the statements of the people involved. Chinese emperors, for example, spoke very ceremonially to their eastern mountain, Tai Shan. In 1572, the nine-year-old Zhu Yijun came to the throne as the fourteenth emperor of the Ming dynasty, received the imperial name Wanli and shortly afterwards addressed Tai Shan:

Foreword

O God, you give birth to everything which must bloom, and you concentrate the supernatural energy in yourself. You are the eternally lasting glory of the oriental lands. You assure the peace of the people and of all beings. Ten thousand generations have really found help from you. Now, through the rights of heredity, I have been invested with supreme power. With deference I perform the rites; oh God, would You accept the sacrifices and listen to the prayers; stand by my dynasty.[6]

A woman from the Peruvian Andes kept it much more informal and laconic. Like many others, María Poma Ticlla was interrogated in 1660 by a Spanish inquisitor who wanted to expose and eradicate the 'idolatry' of the Indigenous population. Under duress, she confessed to occasionally addressing her mountain with a short prayer: 'Antanama Hurco, receive this which we offer to increase the llamas. I wish for it so much.' She fed and gave gifts to the mountain deity with the intention of receiving worldly goods, general help or simply a good life.[7]

Neither of these statements, which are attested by sources, can be understood in isolation from their context. Alone, they remain as enigmatic as many of the self-testimonies of alpinists. What exactly drives them to climb certain mountain peaks faced with huge effort and danger? Take the famous explanation that one has to climb Mount Everest 'because it's there' (George Mallory, 1923). The statement is very open to interpretation. Those approaching it in a historical-critical way should start from the concrete context in which it was made. It is usually difficult to put an unusual goal or experience into words, and one can also read too much into such bon mots. In our case of religious mountain worship, for example, the context consists of pilgrimages, whose historical origins and conjunctures, organisation and lived culture need to be documented. The social event steers the participants and directs their mental energy and attention in certain directions. Motivations usually include opportunities for pleasure and other worldly intentions.

The explanatory value of religious narratives, visions and dogmatic determinations is, from a social and cultural-historical point of view, less than was assumed by older religious studies, still dominated by theological interpretations. The doctrinal edifices often have a complex relationship to the rituals, practices and worldviews of the wider population, which are of most interest to us here. This does not mean that this book focuses exclusively on popular religiosity. What is important is the interaction between elite and popular culture, in which different segments of the population were either able to assert their ideas, or not. Today, one occasionally encounters the idea that holiness in the Christian sphere could be proclaimed 'from below', as it were at will. In reality, there was a hierarchical order to the determination of the sacred. The outcome of discussions and conflicts was not a foregone conclusion but, in the medium and long term, the centres of power often prevailed.

The reference to a place beyond that transcends human experience is often part of the demarcation of the religious from the secular sphere. This transcendental dimension is usually easier to grasp at the level of social authorities, than at that of the broad population. The religious specialists shaped the peoples' desires for wellbeing and long life into a worldview with general explanations and moral rules. In the everyday life of ordinary people, on the other hand, the desires often remained partial and immediate. They pressed for direct fulfilment, but could also change again quickly and were closely interwoven with worldly life.[8] More important than a precise demarcation of sacred and secular meanings is an examination of the entanglements and historical shifts. For example, what is the significance of the British *Alpine Journal*, a leading organ of mountaineering, claiming in 1918 that this modern sport was a religion?[9] By referring to a wider horizon, the forms of perception considered here can be better understood.

How this Book Came About

I have been working on the history of mountain regions for a long time. However, a global, comparative view of the religious aspects only emerged from a special occasion. Together with colleagues from India and Latin America, I was asked to prepare a round table at the Twentieth International Congress of Historical Sciences in Australia in 2005. The committee had given us the theme *Mountain Peoples and Societies: Nature and Culture*. 'Nature and Culture' seemed too European to us, so we fleshed it out with the more globally appropriate isssue of the sacredness of the mountains. This led to a first publication, which was later followed by a general monograph on the comparative history of mountains in the modern era and other studies.[10]

Ideas and impulses also came from the major environment and development conference in Rio de Janeiro in 1992, when mountains were recognised for the first time in an important UN document, the Agenda 21 (for the twenty-first century), as a 'major ecosystem' alongside the oceans and deserts. Among other things, the proponents brought religious arguments into play. Mountains have entered the inner core of societies since the beginning of human history, they said: 'All the major and many minor religions render mountains spiritually significant. And despite the spread of modern scepticism, these emotional, religious or spiritual forces prevail throughout much of the world.' Ignoring them in development policy would therefore mean losing a crucial part of the world's cultural heritage and endangering a critical pillar of our cultural diversity.[11]

It seemed to us at the time that this diversity could be endangered precisely by such generalising and homogenising statements. In any case, it was important for us to take the diversity of mountain religious cultures seriously. That is also an important working hypothesis of this book. How the positions represented here relate to earlier and current theoretical discourses is addressed in the text on a case-by-case basis.

For specific questions that have arisen in the course of the work, I have conducted first-hand research. This was particularly necessary when religious aspects in contemporary discourse were overlooked by the accessible historical literature or were not presented accurately enough. In certain cases, I have also personally contacted specialists; for example, in order to obtain information about a particular Chinese expression. The language is inaccessible to me, and I also lack to some extent the cultural context to judge a statement appropriately. This contextual knowledge is one of the greatest difficulties for a global history of sacred mountains. It can to some extent be solved with reading. The present book is guided by the available scholarly literature published in European languages. Tracking these texts down through widely varied disciplines and remote regions was one of the challenges of the project.

The book is aimed at an interested public, without excluding specialists from different fields. For both, I have striven to use accessible language. For the latter, I have tried to make the bibliographical background accessible in the endnotes.[12] A warm word of thanks goes to all those countless confidants who have enriched me with their knowledge over the years and to the people who assisted me in this book's publication, especially Daniel Anker, Eric T. Hounshell, Jakob Messerli, Alessandro Pastore and Clà Riatsch. 'There are mountains beyond the mountains' is a Chinese saying that a colleague from Beijing passed on to me.[13] According to her, the saying calls for modesty. Behind every mountain (or person) there may be another one that is higher, more beautiful, wiser – and perhaps holier.

A START IN TWO STAGES

~ 1 ~

HOW DOES A SACRED MOUNTAIN COME INTO BEING?

At the root, there are certain words: in Europe *holy, sacred* (English), *heilig* (German), *sacré, saint* (French), *sacro, santo* (Italian, Spanish, Portuguese), etc. Around these core words are layered other words such as the more elevated *sacred* (*sakral, sacrale, sagrado*). Nowadays, it is not difficult to obtain corresponding information from continents beyond Europe. Google offers a globally conceived translation service. At present, more than a hundred languages are available. The translations are used by millions of users, occasionally checked and improved according to their opinion. I have not found one language in Google Translate in which there is no counterpart for sacred: most entries are in the Latin alphabet, but other scripts regularly appear too, for example in Indonesian (*suci*), Xhosa (*ngcwele*) and Samoan (*paia*).[1] Apparently, the word is considered relevant and translatable around the world.

We should not overstate this observation. It is likely that the meaning of *sacred* varies greatly across cultures. Often the translation is probably a makeshift, because expressions that are considered relevant have to be rendered somehow. Artificial links are accepted in the process. The comparative human sciences provide numerous hints in this regard. So far, however, there is no standard overview that would satisfy modern demands and to which we could systematically refer.[2] In Europe, linguistic studies have also attempted to decipher the historical origin of *holy* and to reconstruct the 'original' meaning.[3] For our purposes, this etymological method is of little value. What is of interest here is not speculative beginnings, but the use of the language at a particular point in space and time. For this purpose, let us examine the Tridentine oath formula of the Catholic Creed, issued by a papal bull of 13 November 1564.

Canonisation in European Terms

This oath, the *Professio Fidei Tridentinae*, had to be sworn by all Catholic priests until the twentieth century. It began like this:

How Does a Sacred Mountain Come into Being?

> I N. [name] with firm faith believe and profess and several the things which are contained in the symbol of Faith which the holy Church of Rome doth use, to wit: I believe in One God, the Father Almighty, maker of heaven and of earth, [...] and in one Lord Jesus Christ, the only begotten Son of God, and born of the Father before all time, God of God, Light of Light [...]; and in the holy Ghost, the Lord and giver of Life, who proceedeth from the Father and the Son [...] Amen.

After this time-honoured introduction to the Trinity, the priests had to testify their fidelity to the most important decisions of the Council of Trent, especially to the sources of faith (Tradition of the Holy Church and Holy Scripture) and to the seven sacraments of the new covenant (Order, Baptism, Confirmation, Eucharist, Penance, Extreme Unction and Matrimony). The last part was followed by the promise to render true obedience to the Church, the Pope and the Council and to remain steadfast in the faith 'until the very last gasp of life'.[4]

Recited in the original Latin wording and dignified tone, this oath formula lasted more than five minutes. Apart from the general formula 'heaven and earth', nature and the environment were not addressed in it. Everything revolved around human beings, primarily personally conceived divine beings and the institutions concerned with them. *Holy* occurred sixteen times – for the Roman Church (four times), for the Holy Scriptures (three), for the Council (three), for the saints (three), for the Holy Ghost (two) and for the Eucharist (one). One can assume that it also applied to God the Father and God the Son, but that was not said. The Eucharist, whose holiness seemed already inherent in the notion of sacrament, was additionally designated with the superlative *most holy*.

The concept of the sacred has been a topic of discussion in the Christian Church since its beginnings in late antiquity and has at times been hotly disputed, as in the sixteenth century by Martin Luther and other reformers. The Council of Trent, to which the oath referred, took a stand on this in many ways. Cardinal Marcello Cervini, a papal envoy to the Council, convened a small group of theologians in early 1547 to examine the Reformation writings. Luther had claimed in 1520 that there were only two sacraments, and he seemed to downplay their effectiveness and role in the practice of the faith. Cervini's commission extracted 35 points from the suspect writings that seemed to contradict Catholic teaching. For about four centuries, theology had paid much attention to the sacraments, so there was plenty of reading material on the subject. The points were subsequently discussed in the General Assembly and finally summarised in thirteen articles. On 3 March 1547, the assembly unanimously approved them.[5]

The first article placed under church sanctions any person saying that the sacraments had not been instituted by Jesus Christ, that there were more or fewer than the seven sacraments, or that one of them was not a true sacrament.[6] This was just the beginning. After this general clarification, the Council still had to deal with the individual sacraments, which was particularly difficult and took a long time with the controversial Eucharist. It was necessary to explain and affirm the much-discussed real presence of Christ at the Eucharist and the 'transubstantiation' taking place. Transubstantiation was the name given to the change of essence of the bread and wine used in the ritual into the body and blood of Christ. In addition, there were a number of liturgical points, such as whether the wine chalice should also go to the individual faithful, and how the leftover host, the consecrated bread, should be kept. Indicating the long timespan of these debates, this matter was not decided for convent women until the last session of the Council in December 1563.[7]

The host, the body of Christ, was not only consumed by the faithful and taken into their own bodies. It was also displayed and visually venerated. For this purpose, special demonstration vessels, so-called monstrances, were developed from the late Middle Ages onwards. There seems to have been an increasing desire for worshippers to see it for themselves.[8] Thus, an elaborate monstrance culture spread in the Catholic regions in the sixteenth and seventeenth centuries. Even less well-off parishes and monasteries spent a lot on the vessels, while the wealthier ones could afford precious metal and precious stones. The Great Monstrance of Einsiedeln, completed in 1663, has about 3,000 precious gemstones.[9] The innermost core of these vessels was the opening displaying the host. Among other things, it was referred to as the *Sanctissimum*, the 'Holy of Holies', an expression that otherwise meant the entire sacrament of the Eucharist and emphasised its significance.

The monstrance culture originally arose to display relics of saints. The Council reacted to the Reformation's rejection of this ancient tradition of the saints with a detailed decree. The apostolic church includes the doctrine 'that the saints, who reign at the same time as Christ, offer their intercessions for men to God, and that it is good and useful to invoke them humbly'. Their remains must also be venerated, i.e. 'the holy bodies of the holy martyrs and others living with Christ, who were living members of Christ and a temple of the Holy Ghost'.[10] In 1588, a quarter of a century after the decree of Trent, the canonisation of new (deceased) persons began again after a long interruption. By 1767, when the Vatican discontinued the practice again during the Enlightenment period, 55 persons had posthumously attained sainthood. Many of them were men (42), members of religious orders (38), Italians (27), nobles (at least 26) and Spaniards (17). 'It is obvious enough that the 55 men and women were not a random sample from the Catholic population at large', comments cultural historian Peter Burke.[11]

In fact, centralised ecclesiastical control and administrative hurdles for canonisation were constantly being expanded. Local saints or unconventional candidates had a harder time than before. Sainthood was considered a 'heroic virtue' that now had to be proven in detail through evidence of an appropriate lifestyle, authenticated miracles, etc. Many proposals got stuck in the Roman hierarchy.[12] Of interest here is the fact that the saints continued to have a semi-mobile character. While their gravesites had special significance, their remains were transferable as relics and independent of location. This is another indication that the 'topography of the sacred' had a distinctly human character and environmental elements played only a minor role in it. This peculiar absence of nature had been in place since the institutionalisation of Christianity in late antiquity.[13] To change the situation, new, strong forces were needed, as will be discussed later.

To sum up our initial examination: as a model for the emergence of holy mountains, the section of the European Catholic path considered so far proves unproductive. In this respect, the Protestant-Evangelical path also deviated only slightly for the time being.[14] A look at other parts of the world is much more helpful.

Tibetan Mountain Rituals

Between about 1570 and 1575 – shortly after the Council of Trent and the aforementioned bull – the Buddhist monk Pema Karpo wrote a mythological guidebook to the Pure Crystal Mountain (Dakpa Sheri) in south-eastern Tibet. The mountain district called Tsari, carved by deep valleys, has a main peak of 5,735 metres and lies on the border with Assam, where the Tibetan highlands drop steeply into the southern rainforest. Today, the provisional China-India border, the McMahon Line, is located there. Karpo's guidebook was not the first text on this particular mountain, but it soon found wide circulation and became a widely read and remembered long-term classic.[15] Writing possesses medieval ancestry in Tibet. Religious texts circulated in the form of manuscripts and so-called block prints. In block printing, an entire (later paper) page was carved out of a wooden panel in reverse. The monasteries had large storehouses where thousands of such wooden plates for each page of a work were kept and used for reprinting books when needed.

The Pure Crystal Mountain guidebook was entitled *Verse Eulogy to the Holy Place of Tsari* (in Tibetan, *Tsa ri tra zhes pa'i gnas la bstod pas pad dkar legs bshad*). It consisted of a mixture of prayers, religious polemics, cosmology, esoteric ritual prescriptions, Tantric Buddhist geography, anecdotes and historical narratives, mostly taken from older sources and all in verse form, so as to be more memorable. For example, the story is told of a Buddhist master who worships the mountain by means of walking around it and attains supernormal abilities from mountain deities in meditation. In his right hand the master takes a powerful magical plant, in his left he holds his walking stick; then he begins to dance and chants the following:

> This supreme *né* [holy mountain], glorious Tsari / Is not wandered by all and sundry / I have abandoned worldly activities / I have self-luminosity of mind itself // It's a place to fling down life and limb / It's a place to remove hindrances whose causes are outer and inner / It's a place to make an analysis of cyclic existence / It's a place to weigh ascetics (and their accomplishments) in the balance.[16]

The author, Pema Karpo (1527–1592), was considered a great scholar and storyteller. He came from the regional lower nobility and was identified as the fourth reincarnation of the founder of the Drukpa sect, which formed the leading religious community on the Tsari pilgrimage routes. He was writing at a time when pilgrimage was greatly increasing, and a new phase of mountain worship was beginning. It is believed that the mountain – like many others in Tibet – was first worshipped on a local scale. Such cults of the so-called *yül-lha* type ('god of the locale') were associated with local communities and their identity. They were transmitted orally and their periodic rituals at the foot of the sacred mountains addressed immediate desires and problems of ordinary life. Then, from the late twelfth century, during a period of expansion of Buddhist sects, wandering ascetics seem to have established the religious power of Tsari by means of Tantric meditation. It rose to become a mountain of the *néri* type ('mountain abode of important deities'). This cult form was also about questions of death and future life on the path to enlightenment, whether as rebirth or subsequent liberation from it. It was embedded in Buddhist text traditions and was supported by religious specialists, and its followers comprised regional and supra-regional people.[17]

For the establishment of Tsari as a most sacred mountain, meditation with spatial mandala models was of particular importance. The hermits and wandering ascetics thus produced a visionary religious landscape that could be

How Does a Sacred Mountain Come into Being?

fixed to many points of the outer landscape and preferably concerned places where famous spiritual pioneers had brought precious 'treasures' to light by these means. In time, the mountain's growing reputation gave rise to a popular pilgrimage. It seems that magic did not fail to impact the interpersonal sphere either. The various routes around the mountain were fixed in the sixteenth century, among others by the aforementioned guidebook of Pema Karpo. The main pilgrimage ritual of the Crystal Mountain, known as the 'great ravine circuit of Tsari' (*Tsari Rongkor Chenmo*), then developed in the eighteenth century in parallel with the solidification of the theocratic state in central Tibet. The earlier meditation traditions had largely disappeared by then and were only revived in the twentieth century.[18]

The 'great ravine circuit' was a dramatic and dangerous mass procession that took place every twelve years until 1956, during the Tibetan Years of the Monkey. Dangers resulted from the necessary descent into the impassable jungles of the south and from the small tribal societies that dominated this area and were often hostile to the Buddhist pilgrims. The 1944 procession even resulted in a massacre. Pilgrims flocked from all parts of Tibet each time, usually numbering around 20,000 people. In order to be able to hold the event despite adverse conditions, envoys from Lhasa used to pay a 'barbarian tribute' to tribal leaders before the circumambulation began. By means of the gift ritual, performed with much ceremonial effort and affirmed by an oath, the Buddhist elite hoped to provide safe conduct for their people. But even without any encroachments, the procession of a good 150 kilometres, taking about two weeks to complete, was exceedingly demanding. And only those who completed the circumambulation with devotion in the spirit of Buddha could hope for the atonement of sins and religious merit.[19]

The authorities in Lhasa invested heavily in this sacred mountain district and its mass procession. The connection was symbolically underlined by the fact that pilgrims prominently carried items of clothing belonging to the Dalai Lama through the ravine circuit each time. More than elsewhere, religiously motivated restrictions on use were also imposed. Around the Pure Crystal Mountain, all life and substances were considered sacred or divine. The authorities prohibited any agricultural cultivation of the land. Clearing for grazing or keeping pigs and chickens that might stir up and disturb the soil were also forbidden. Taboos included, of course, the hunting and killing of all living creatures. The disposal of human excreta was also strictly regulated on the circumambulation routes.[20]

Figure 1. Tibetan scroll painting of the Pure Crystal Mountain as a shrine with pilgrims (hand-painted).

How Does a Sacred Mountain Come into Being?

The history of Tsari has been impressively researched by Toni Huber, tibetologist and anthropologist working on Tibetan environmental perception, who summarises:

> It is a well-known feature of Tibetan culture, both pre-modern and contemporary, that the physical environment in both its animate and inanimate dimensions is believed to be occupied by a host of deities and spirit forces. They range from minor autochthons to supreme Tantric deities and Buddhas, and can exist in the world-space as a totality, by pervading all things in various ways, or reside at specific locations, being both mobile and fixed.[21]

The deities thus inhabit certain mountains and other landscape elements and embody themselves in them, so that the natural elements have an independent divine character. The Tibetan term *gnas* (sacred) and its compounds can refer to divine dwellings in all modes of existence, as personal beings as well as physical elements. Unlike in early modern Europe, where nature was excluded from sacredness, the aforementioned categories for sacred and highly sacred mountains (*yüllha*, *néri*) were also known.[22]

Arbitrary Sacredness?

Toni Huber was already familiar with the language and scriptures as a tibetologist when he became able to do field research from the 1980s and participated in more than a dozen different pilgrimages in Tibet. At that time, China loosened its political control over the 'Autonomous Region' for a while and opened the borders. Among the first foreigners to receive permission to go on pilgrimage in Tibet was Reinhold Messner, an extreme mountaineer and adventurer from South Tyrol. He had already climbed most of the world's fourteen eight-thousanders without the aid of bottled oxygen and had become very famous for his books and media appearances. In Tibet in 1985, he was drawn to the holy Mount Kailash, the 'mountain of all mountains', as he calls it. For the time being, he simply mingled with the pilgrims who were circling the mountain for religious reasons.

Later, the sanctity of the mountains also gained importance in Messner's performance-oriented life. From 1997, he filmed several episodes of the series *Abodes of the Gods* (*Wohnungen der Götter*) with German Television. After the turn of the millennium, starting from his Juval Castle in South Tyrol, he began a large-scale museum project on the relationship between mountains and humans, including the religious and spiritual aspects. In 2013, his *My Sacred Mountains* (*Meine heiligen Berge*) was published, with pictures and partly autobiographical texts. This volume is of interest to us for several reasons: Messner has travelled on all continents and has immense mountain experience. He does not deal with the question of sacredness from the point of view of a scientific expert (like Toni Huber, for example), but with informed general knowledge and with an eye to Western public taste. That gives us a certain system of coordinates.[23] 'Mountains have always been sacred to people', promises the blurb:

> Not because they had a religion, but because nature was sacred to them. They approached it with reverence, which was later expressed in the fact that the mountains were considered the seat of the gods, to which no mortal had access. They were also seen as the bridge between heaven and earth, between God and man.

For the reader 'a window opens into a strange world whose fascination is hard to resist'. This indicates that, in Messner's opinion, the sacred is to be sought more in the remote past and in foreign lands than in the familiar Alpine, Christian environment. The tendency to refer to past epochs for this purpose becomes particularly clear in the book's South American example, the Licancábur volcano in the Atacama Desert. According to Messner, this volcano is one of the most important sanctuaries in the Andes, as can be seen from the Inca material remains found there, dating from the fourteenth and fifteenth centuries. However, direct references to an associated, clearly tangible mountain cult in history and the present are not offered – the bar is set low.[24]

Messner is unequivocal about the culture in which he grew up: 'Mountains were never sacred to Christians.' Only when a salvation event took place on them, as on Mount Sinai, could one consider them holy in a limited sense. 'In contrast, the peaks of the Himalayas have always been thought of as the dancing place of the gods, an image I can still follow today.'[25] This European–Asian comparison aims in the same direction as our previous observations on Catholic canonisation and Tibetan mountain rituals. However, Messner (as a representative of widespread opinions) still finds ambivalent beings occasionally making an appearance under the official Christian blanket: 'In Central Europe, mountains were the territory of ghosts, witches and monsters.' Their exact role in the historical dramaturgy of the sacred is not explained, however. This also applies to Ötzi, the prehistoric 'Iceman', in whose discovery Messner personally played a role in 1991. With imagination and little evidence, the museum at Juval Castle is staged as 'Ötzi's cult place'.[26]

Can we judge the sacredness of a mountain by its shape or by the view from its summit? Messner poses the often-raised question on an elegant volcano in Africa and in front of a series of strikingly shaped mountains in Arizona.[27] It becomes clear that the physical landscape cannot provide any

How Does a Sacred Mountain Come into Being?

real answers. Ultimately, clarification is required as to whether the shape also appears impressive to the locals and could perhaps have contributed to a cult practice. This intensive attention to the people and the historical evidence on the ground was not among Messner's strengths. He was often in a hurry. On his first trip to Japan, for example, he was pressed for time, but still managed to squeeze an ascent of the famous sacred national mountain Fujiyama into his programme 'as a kind of cultural trip'. Disappointment followed on its heels. Messner saw 'nothing magical', the trip was 'neither spectacular nor mysterious'. On a second occasion, he prepared himself and climbed the national mountain with thousands of Japanese pilgrims during the main season. What he remembers most are the countless digital cameras trying to capture the atmosphere at sunrise. Can such a mountain (still) be sacred? That is the telling, but unanswered question at the end.[28]

Messner's book repeatedly pleads for reverence for mountains and nature – a reverence that he also attributes to the *Naturvölker* (primitive peoples) and sees disappearing in 'materialistic' Western modernity. One could try to locate this concept of reverence in the religious-spiritual field of the West.[29] Here, I would only like to contextualise the *Naturreligion* (nature religion) mentioned in the book. The term comes from the inventory of European imperialism. *Meyers Konversation-Lexikon* of 1888, for example, stated that *Naturreligion* stood in contrast to cultural religion. It was the religion of so-called primitive peoples, with no real history. However, those peoples did not represent the unadulterated origin of humanity either, since 'their present condition rather often appears as degeneration and savagery'.[30] While the dictionary used the term 'primitive' in the strongly pejorative sense of imperialist superiority, Messner – like many others of his generation – reassessed the judgement. Primitive peoples and natural religions are now conversely high in value.

However, the majority of modern scholarship finds that the term 'nature religion' is still misleading per se – not only because of the implicit nature–culture opposition, but also because one does not observe religious reference to nature as a whole in the small societies concerned, but to specific elements of it. 'Nature' is an abstract European word with a long history, an expression of practised worldviews. Today, *ethnic religion* or *Indigenous religion* are proposed instead of *nature religion* – though these are terms that are worthy of interrogation too.[31]

The Desert Fathers

In 2010, Messner spent a week searching for the biblical Mount Sinai in the rocky desert of the same name in Egypt. The starting point was Saint Catherine's

The Desert Fathers

Monastery at the foot of Mount Horeb, where the God of the Torah and the Bible is said to have handed the Ten Commandments to Moses, the leader of Israel. Messner experienced the climb as a 'revelation' in a critical sense. He recalled that Mount Sinai, which is mentioned in the Scriptures, could not be located definitively, and he considered the monotheism apparently founded here. The faith in one God, in his view, leads to a monopoly on truth and morality and has a violent character. It elevates itself above the *Naturreligionen*, which means that the mountains lose their charisma. Mount Sinai would be just another mountain for Christians if the triune God had not occasionally taken possession of it.[32]

UNESCO takes a different view, and added the 'Saint Catherine Area' including the Christian Orthodox monastery and Mount Horeb to the World Heritage List in 2002. The entire area is classified as 'sacred' for three 'world religions' (Christianity, Judaism and Islam) according to the guidelines of the corresponding international convention. Founded in the sixth century, the monastery is the oldest Christian institution of its kind still in operation to this day. Built in a remote location at over 1,500 metres, it shows an intimate relationship between 'natural grandeur and spiritual commitment'.[33]

The question for us is how old this 'greatness' or 'sublimity' of nature could be. According to specialists in late antiquity, it was not at the origin of the ascetic-monastic movement that spread in this region from the late third century onwards. Hermits and ascetics, sometimes united in monastic communities, segregated themselves in the sparsely populated desert to escape from the intense social life of the Nile Valley. 'The overwhelming impression given by the literature of the early Egyptian ascetics, is that we are dealing with men who found themselves driven into the desert by a crisis in human relations', notes ancient historian Peter Brown. It was about finding a place for undisturbed self-discovery and seeking God in the struggle with one's own sins and 'demons'.[34] Even though the desert was only the setting, it shaped a religious metaphor that was to become part of the monastic identity for a very long time. The 'Desert Fathers' were pioneers of Christian monastic life. Abbeys that were located in the mountains could also be seen as being in the desert.[35]

This strongly institutionalised attitude towards nature can be seen most clearly at the Grande Chartreuse, an enclosed Alpine valley at an altitude of 1,200 metres near Grenoble, France. In the High Middle Ages, hermits retreated to this remote area and soon formed a monastic community. It was the first monastery of the Carthusian Order, which imposed a strict, silent lifestyle in solitary cells. After the order's *fuga mundi* (flight from the world) had gained

How Does a Sacred Mountain Come into Being?

widespread popularity in Europe, its founder, Bruno of Cologne, was canonised in 1514. At that time, the mountain valley near Grenoble had already become a sacred district, which began to be marked with Christian crosses. It was generally regarded as the 'Desert of the Great Chartreuse' (*Désert de la Grande Chartreuse*), a term derived from the ascetics and Desert Fathers of late antiquity. The derivation formed the core of self-perception and self-representation. Desert usually came before mountain. 'It is a terrible place, a dreadful desert, far from all habitation, from all help', reads a hagiography of 1788: 'For company one has here only the animals. The surroundings consist of extremely high mountains which touch the clouds; of barren, craggy rocks which make one fear an imminent landslide which will destroy everything.' While such images of terror underlined the heroism of the founder and his successors, in other depictions the desert mutated into a Garden of Eden, whose pleasantness was due to the holiness of the monks.[36]

Monasteries are usually places with a surplus of ideas. Their names may not follow the common language, and may be freighted with a cultural background. It is therefore probably not entirely coincidental that we find traditions in Asia in which a monastery appears as a 'mountain' regardless of its location. The Zen Buddhist system of Five Mountains and Ten Temples (Chinese: *Wushan Shicha*, Japanese: *Gozan Jissetsu Seido*) originated in southern China in the early days of the Grande Chartreuse, and spread to the whole of Japan from the late thirteenth century. At that time, it was closely linked to the ruling shogunate and formed a hierarchical administrative order. The highest rank was held by the monasteries of the Five Mountains, then came those of the Ten Temples, and the rest were assigned to a third category.[37] Even after their heyday, this designation persisted. A famous monastery of the highest category that still exists is Nanzen-ji on the eastern edge of Kyoto. When I was there a few years ago, it would never have occurred to me without reading up on this that there could also be 'mountain monasteries' in the flat urban area.

Revolutionary Symbolism

Back to our question: how does a sacred mountain come into being? In the case of Tibet – as we have seen – one can assume a cumulative process that can partly be reconstructed from historical sources. Buddhist ascetics used natural elements, and mountains in particular, for their meditative practices. The aura they developed attracted followers and, over time, gave rise to institutionalised pilgrimages. As the older local mountain cults in Tibet show, they did this on a cultural basis that included nature in religious perception from the outset.[38]

Revolutionary Symbolism

Precisely this basis was not present in Christianity and, as far as we know, had not been since its institutionalisation in late antiquity. In the literature, the fading out of nature by the early church is usually conflated with its urban origins and its rise as a simultaneously harassed and contentious community in the Roman Empire. Both circumstances are likely to have encouraged the conspicuous focus on human relationships. The conspiratorial, hierarchically-organised church was inward-looking and may also have downplayed the importance of natural elements to set itself apart from competing faiths.[39] In its main features, the topography of the sacred thus contoured then persisted for a very long time.[40] The lasting influence of historical events on the religious field is shown by the modern mountain monasteries, which were derived from the 'Desert Fathers' of late antiquity and inhabited *déserts*.

As a contrasting foil to Buddhist and oither perceptions, Christianity is of no small interest for the question of sacred mountains. Cult forms that point to the transition to modernity can also be examined particularly well. As we will see in Chapter 2, the emergence of natural history in Europe from the sixteenth century onwards played a central role in the change of perception. 'Nature' thus became an important theme in literature and the arts, and a moral model of the primordial and unaffected. Against this backdrop, the period of the French Revolution saw a sharp politicisation of nature, which briefly gave rise to a kind of holy mountains. This is another model for the emergence of *Mount Sacred* – extra-religious and as a passing fad.

The revolution was underway and gaining momentum; in Paris, the king had lost part of his power when the National Assembly got involved in a dispute over the political use of the term 'mountain' at the end of October 1791. A little later, for reasons that are not entirely clear, the expressions 'mountain' and 'mountain people' (*montagne, montagnards*) referred to a radical political grouping and its partisans. By 1793, the terms had become common, apparently also because the *montagnards* were seated in the upper rows of the old conference hall, while the moderate faction sat below in the 'plain' (*plaine*). There was a moral tension between the two: mountains were considered pure and mountain people virtuous, whereas the plain could also be a 'swamp' (*marais*). These polemical concepts of nature were constantly used in songs, plays and newspapers.[41]

At the same time, revolutionaries began to use artificially created mountains to embody nature in their new ritual and festival culture. In the capital and in the provinces, piles of earth were erected or hill-like, often walk-in, settings were built with makeshift theatre architecture, both outdoors and in churches, from which the Christian symbols had been removed in the wake of anti-clerical policies. Some of these artificial *montagnes sacrées*, as they were also called, were more than ten metres high. The mountain that was heaped up on the Champ de Mars (Field of Mars; in front of today's Eiffel Tower) to celebrate the 'Supreme Being' on 8 June 1794 became famous (Figure 2). At the top stood an altar dedicated to the fatherland and a tree of liberty. The population was required to pay homage to the *Être suprême* according to gender and age, among other things by singing a hymn. In the text, the 'Father of the Universe' with his temple on the mountains revealed the essence of nature to the people and they implored him to strengthen the fatherland in hatred of the kings.[42]

Figure 2. Hill raised on the Champ de Mars in Paris to worship the Supreme Being, 1794 (coloured engraving).

There is little doubt that this led to a certain sacralisation of nature and the mountains. One widely read author, for example, published a 'catechism of nature' and designed a 'natural religion and morality'.[43] Modern scholars speak of a transfer of sacrality from the Christian to the new social context, but also of a mixture of the most diverse cultural patterns.[44] Compared to earlier forms of cult, the revolutionary upsurge had a decidedly national character. It can be seen as a harbinger of a time in which the secular nation state was sometimes canonised. The artificial mountains, on the other hand, quickly

Revolutionary Symbolism

became obsolete. After a bloody wave of executions, they were described as 'monuments of terror' in the National Convention of 1795. The Convention debated whether they should be destroyed or preserved out of respect for the people, so as not to give the aristocrats cause for gloating. One deputy finally interjected that he could very well recognise the mountains as a symbol of the people if they were not also a cause for division: 'A mountain, is it not an eternal revolt against equality?' The Convention then decided to remove all artificial mountains from the territory of the Republic and ordered a new parliamentary seating arrangement.[45]

~ 2 ~

A WORLD BETWEEN FAITH AND KNOWLEDGE

This chapter looks at the way faith and knowledge have intertwined in the East and West since the end of the Middle Ages. It is an orientation guide for the site visits to selected sacred mountains, the destination of this book. It also includes the historical pedigree of the views that we encounter today. How should the many signs of this world be correctly interpreted? Two framework conditions played an important role in the perception of nature and the ways this changed in modern times: urbanisation and territorial expansion. The emergence of large cities favoured the division of labour and specialisation; religious and scientific discourses could be set in motion more easily with the more numerous opportunities for contact than were available in small settlements and towns. Territorial expansion, on the other hand, whether in the form of individual exploration or state-led seizure, promoted comparative observations of cultural and natural matters. What previously had general validity could turn out, through the expansion of the horizon of perception, to be a special case, and vice versa.[1]

In the early twentieth century, London was the largest city in the world, with a population of about 6.5 million, and the British Empire claimed a quarter of the global land area. Expansion began in the sixteenth century and, especially in the nineteenth century, led to a territory more than a hundred times larger than the British Isles, where the colonial grip originated. The situation was different in eastern Eurasia, especially at the beginning of the modern era. Around 1500, Beijing had about 700,000 inhabitants, surpassing any other city on the globe at that time. The population of China, then under the rule of the Ming Dynasty, accounted for one fifth to one quarter of the world's population. It is estimated as having been a good hundred million, while the British Isles had a population of barely four million. In the following centuries, the Middle Kingdom retained this extraordinary demographic weight.[2] The role the empire accorded to its mountains was also special. This Chinese conception is our first topic here; afterwards we will follow the European line of tradition, which finally points back to Asia.

Chinese Mountain Systematics

> I had been devoted to the Five Sacred Mountains for a long time, and coming to Ta-liang [now Kaifang, Henan Province], I was determined to travel to the Middle Sacred Mountain one day. Just at that time, we had a blazing hot summer, and people said it was not very pleasant to go up. Although many tried to dissuade me, I brushed all concerns aside.

So, the Chinese scholar P'an Lei ignored the advice he had been given, and on 10 July 1701 began a ten-day journey into the Sung Shan, with its rugged topography and numerous peaks. He hired a team of palanquin bearers and purchased a copy of *Chronicle of the Mountain,* published in 1668, in order to get an idea of the sights and the various religious and cultural merits of the place. It became a temple tour: Sacrificial Temple of the Sacred Middle Mountain, Temple of Sublime Fortune, Temple Monastery of the Dragon Pond, there was also a nunnery – more than a dozen spiritual institutions in all, each with their collections of antiquities. At the end, P'an Lei expressed his satisfaction: 'Walking around like this, admiring the landscape and looking at everything closely, I felt in harmony with the earth.' At the Dragon Pond, the scholar would have liked to 'read prayers and fast on a full moon night. I couldn't get enough of it.' All in all, he combined the pleasure of the landscape with his insatiable appetite for history.[3]

P'an Lei (1646–1708) had taken an early interest in history, phonology and mathematics, and, without passing the usual examinations, obtained a post at the Imperial Academy in Beijing. After being dismissed from there for misconduct, he devoted himself to his own writings and travelled the east and south of the country.[4] Unlike most of his contemporaries, he had already visited more than one sacred state mountain. There were five of them, all between 1,300 and 2,000 metres high: Tai Shan in the east of the empire, Héng Shan in the south, Hua Shan in the west, Heng Shan in the north – and Sung Shan in the middle. In its sacrificial temple, P'an Lei could admire the shrines of all the deities of the 'Five Great Peaks' during his visit.[5] According to a stone stele, the god of Sung Shan bore the family name Yun and the personal name Yang. The imperial house had given the mountain a lofty title, Zhongtian chong shengdi ('High, Holy God of the Middle Mountain'). The mountain also had two assistant mountains (Niu-ki and Chao-ch). The other four were similarly endowed. The stele listed them all, headed with the statement: 'The Five Peaks are considered the most divine thing in the universe.'[6]

A World between Faith and Knowledge

As far as we know, this large-scale territorial system of prominent sacred mountains was unique in the world. In the course of its long history, it was also adapted by certain Chinese tributary states (such as areas in Korea and Yunnan), but it does not seem to have spread further. The empire also employed the 'enfeoffment of mountains', that is, their recognition as vassal peaks, as a means of foreign policy. At times, this network stretched from Japan across Java to southern India. Although the topic has been studied again and again over the centuries, and especially by modern researchers, many questions remain unanswered to this day. Scholarly and religious controversies seem to have accompanied the system since its beginnings. In China, there were numerous mountain cults and thus a great potential for site competition between different peaks or mountains (usually they were groups of peaks; P'an Lei visited only part of the massif on Sung Shan, for example). The earliest writings merely stated the general religious-geographical scheme; it was commented on and localised by later scholars, each with their own interests.[7]

The system is thought to have emerged from a combination of early state and territory formation with a substrate of local mountain cults. At first, there was only talk of four major peaks and, at times, of other ensembles. With the emergence of the empire in the last pre-Christian centuries, the number five was consolidated, which at that time was also considered favourable and significant in the five-element philosophy. It was a symbolic marking of Chinese territory. In research, the neologism *marchmounts*, landmark mountains, has also been brought into play. *Wuyue* is the name given to the category of five sacred, famous or great peaks in Chinese.[8] The Wuyue had a place in the state ritual calendar observed by the emperor as the 'Son of Heaven', and were thus included in the system of government. In practice, the sacrifices to be made were usually delegated. With their assigned titles, the mountains received, as it were, public offices. Neglect or explicit elevation of the titles indicated how the current *power of place* (James Robson's term) stood in the general hierarchy and cultural power structure.[9]

The emperor cult not only corresponded with the five-element doctrine, which described the five basic elements of wood, fire, metal, water and earth and their five phases of transformation. It was also connected with cosmic mythologies of origins. When the primordial figure of Pangu died through self-sacrifice after thousands of years of life, the universe was formed from his body. According to one version, the Tai Shan, the most prominent of the Wuyue, emerged from the Pangu's head, and the other four from lower parts of the body.[10] At the popular level, the cult led to extensive pilgrimages. P'an

Chinese Mountain Systematics

Lei observed in 1701 at Middle Mountain that almost as many pilgrims turned up for the important festivals in spring as at Tai Shan. According to his judgement, the pilgrims behaved more demurely here than at the East Mountain. Instead of throwing themselves into the miracle belief of the mountain deity as if under a spell, they immersed themselves more in prayers. Talismans with the 'image of the true form of the five peaks' were also important for the population; these could be carried as a paper rubbing of a stone stele (Figure 3) or as a metal amulet to protect life and limb.[11]

Figure 3. 'Image of the true form of the five peaks', China c. 1614 (paper rubbing).

A World between Faith and Knowledge

China's three normative traditions – Confucianism, Daoism and Buddhism – were all represented at the sacred mountains and, despite intermittent conflicts, interacted with each other. Buddhism, introduced to China from India in the early centuries CE, became concentrated on those mountains which, since the reign of Emperor Wanli (1572–1620), have been classified as the 'Four Great Buddhist Peaks'; previously, three such mountains had been spoken of. This system indicates that Indian teachings were now fully absorbed into the culture of the empire. Using the time-honoured genre of mountain-related country descriptions (*mountain gazetteers*), the Chinese historian Kai Sheng has summarised the Buddhist preferences in keywords. Important elements for the selected mountains were: mention in classical texts; landscape and viewpoints; miracle stories; pilgrimages of the faithful; pagodas, temples and outstanding monks; state support.[12]

As previously mentioned, the scholar P'an Lei had many fields of interest, ranging from history to mathematics. At Sung Shan in 1701, he encountered not only numerous temples and monasteries, but also an academy. The building had a chequered history as a religious institution and Confucian teaching centre. After being destroyed, it was rebuilt and attracted many young scholars, thanks to a famous director. One should not think of academic culture as static. In any case, P'an Lei was also a critical spirit, and in his report he questioned certain cult objects on the Middle Mountain that he considered superstitious.[13] In his time, scholarly culture was on the rise. Under the 'enlightened' fourth emperor of the Qing dynasty, Kangxi (reigned 1661–1722), for example, cartography underwent a significant expansion and clarification. In 1708, the year of P'an Lei's death, a new, long-term mapping campaign began with the help of European Jesuits, which soon included Tibet. This resulted in a comprehensive, modern map series, in which the mountain later called Mount Everest, the highest on earth, appeared for the first time.[14]

Sacred Science in Europe

In the same year 1708, the scholarly Latin work *Ouresiphoitēs Helveticus, sive Itinera Alpina Tria* ('Helvetic Mountain Hiker, or Three Journeys through the Alps') was published in London under the auspices of the Royal Society and its president Isaac Newton. In it, the Zurich city physician and naturalist Johann Jakob Scheuchzer (1672–1733) published research reports on mountain journeys he had undertaken with students for about three weeks each in 1702, 1703 and 1704. The book continued sixteenth-century traditions, but also formed a milestone in the emerging European mountain research. One can

Sacred Science in Europe

place Scheuchzer at the beginning of a line in this field that later led to Albrecht von Haller, Horace-Bénédict de Saussure and Alexander von Humboldt. In what follows, I outline the natural history research of the eighteenth century, the alpinism of the nineteenth century and the emerging religious studies of the twentieth century. I refer to points of contact between religious ideas and scientific or physical activities that would be considered profane today. Particular attention is given to the attributions of meaning and their change.

As a prelude to his research initiative, Scheuchzer had a questionnaire printed with around 200 questions and sent it out to informants. Travellers rightly perceive mountainous Switzerland as 'rough and wild', he wrote in the introduction. However, it offered 'great wonders and magnificent gifts of nature' that demanded to be studied in depth.[15] The city physician was, among other things, a pioneer of altitude measurement by means of barometers, which had been experimented with in Europe for decades. His seemingly boundless thirst for knowledge was also religiously motivated. By exploring the 'unbelievable mountain wonders', he said he wanted to praise God as their creator and encourage others to praise God.[16]

In modern research, Scheuchzer is attributed to physico-theology, which emerged in the second half of the seventeenth century and valued external nature for its relationship with religious questions. His last work bore the eloquent title *Copper Bible, in which the Physica Sacra or Sacred Science of the Natural Things occurring in the Holy Scripture is clearly explained* (*Kupfer-Bibel, in welcher die Physica Sacra oder Geheiligte Natur-Wissenschaft derer in Heiligen Schrift vorkommenden Natürlichen Sachen deutlich erklärt wird*). Published from 1731 to 1735, the volumes were richly illustrated with copper engravings (hence 'Copper Bible'), and showed how religious and scientific truths complemented each other. To Exodus, chapter 19, for example, Scheuchzer added information about the behaviour of eagles (mentioned metaphorically in the Bible text about Mount Sinai). Then he commented on the question of whether the mountain, smoking and flashing through God's activity, could be a volcano. In passing, he also referred to the 'idolatries common among the heathen'.[17] For Christians, distancing themselves from heathen mountain-worship was indicated in such cases. Because nature became a testimony to divine creation in his emphatic manner, he was suspected by orthodox opponents of wanting to introduce un-Christian ideas.[18]

In 1746, a German version of the *Itinera Alpina* was published by the Swiss clergyman Johann Georg Sulzer (1720–1779). Scheuchzer had exchanged ideas with the most famous naturalists of his time, the preface stated, and they had given the sciences new prestige: 'They announced war on the old fantasies. They wanted to have a physics whose propositions were founded in the most certain occurrences of nature.'[19] The translator himself had undertaken a journey through the Alps and had devised a new method of barometric elevation measurement. At the end of the new edition, he added his own 'Investigation of the Origin of the Mountains' ('Untersuchung über den Ursprung der Berge'). In it, he gave a stringent summary of the European controversy that had been waged over the history of the earth since the late seventeenth century. Ultimately, the question was how the research corresponded with the biblical creation narrative. Sulzer proposed an original variant of his own. Newton's theory and recent French measurements had shown that the earth was flattened towards the poles. According to him, when the earth began to rotate at the beginning of creation ('Let there be light!'), the sphere must have become an ellipsoid. This had led to tectonic shifts and the inequality of the Earth's surface (Figure 4).[20]

Sulzer was an ordained Protestant pastor. At the same time as his scientific work, he published an *Attempt at Some Moral Reflections on the Works of Nature* (*Versuch einiger moralischen Betrachtungen über die Werke der Natur*). In its entire arrangement, nature points to God as its creator. Even the mountains are only apparently purposeless. Mankind owes to them a great variety of stones and metals, water sources and rivers, as well as the most beautiful and useful plants. The writing was introduced by a Royal Church Councillor (*Königlicher Kirchenrat*) of Frederick II of Prussia. The sciences, physics first and foremost, were extremely useful for the knowledge of God, he stated.[21] For Sulzer, the preface was also a step towards Berlin, where he later made a career as a professor of mathematics and philosophy.[22]

The Lutheran pastor of Schöneck in the Saxon Erzgebirge was more interested in religious practice with his *Orotheology, or Edifying Contemplation on the Mountains* (*Orotheologie, oder erbauliche Betrachtung über die Berge*), published in 1756. He began with the two Christian books: the 'main book' is the book of Revelation or the Holy Scriptures. The 'secondary book' of nature, however, was also necessary, as it pointed to its own path to God. The publication joined the ranks of special theologies that had appeared in Germany on individual elements of nature: frogs and tadpoles (1724), stones (1735), flowers (1737), insects (1738), snails and shells (1744), grasshoppers (1748/1750), grass (1750) and others.[23] As the title announced, the *Orotheology* had an edifying character above all. At the end it offered a prayer, which became quite metaphorical after some biblical quotations: the fruitfulness that the Lord gives to the mountains should not only work outwardly in the congregation, but also inwardly, 'so that

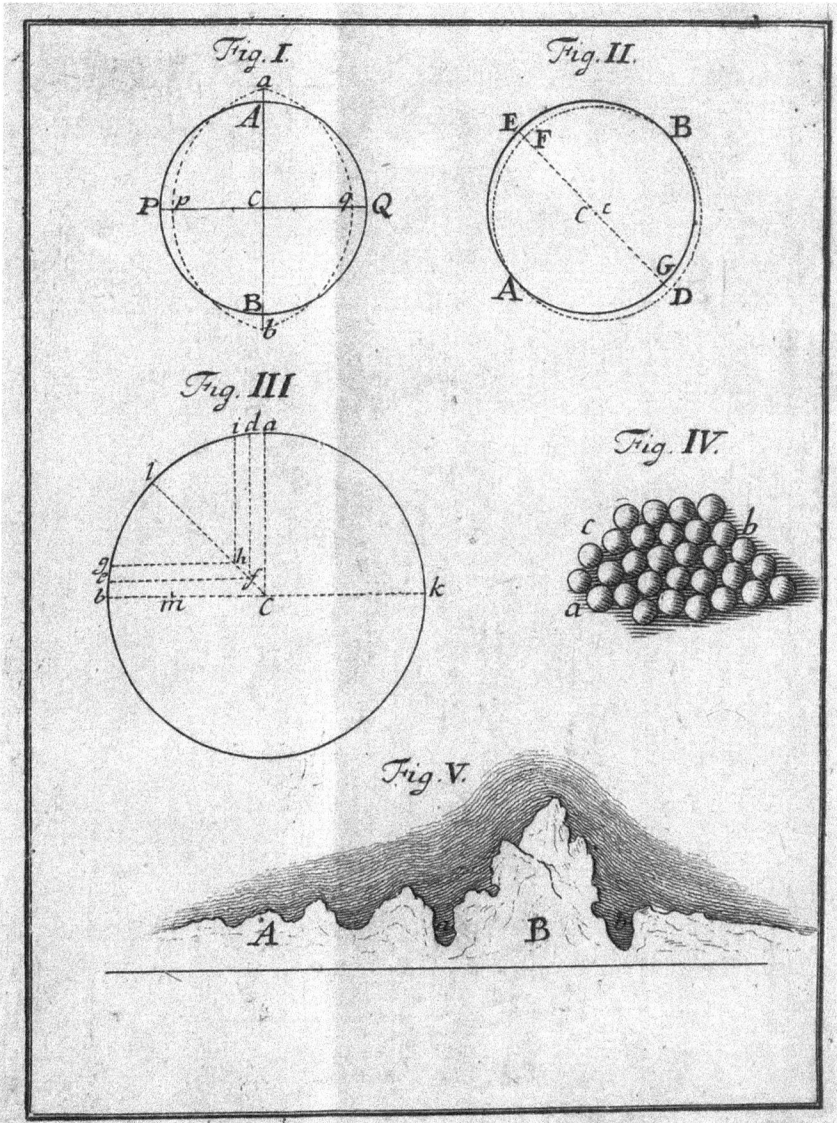

Figure 4. Graphic explanations of the theory of the origin of the mountains by Johann Georg Sulzer, 1746 (engraving).

we may always be pleasant mountains in Your eyes, and as the right mountains of God, on and near which You have Your delight to dwell'.[24]

Physico-theologians often justified their intense preoccupation with nature by pointing out that in this way one could also convince unbelievers of the existence of the Christian God. In the case of mountains, there was sometimes also the fear that their admiration could be confused with pagan mountain worship. 'The heathens used to regard quite a few mountains as deities', *Zedler's Universal-Lexikon* noted in 1733, referring to Roman antiquity and leaving no doubt that this was idolatry for Christians.[25] We have observed that Western Christianity traditionally had an anthropocentric-introverted character and largely ignored nature (see Chapter 1). Driven by the emerging natural sciences, it now began to open up towards the environment and to grant it a religious value.[26]

Mountain Research and Alpinism

In the literature, one often reads that the mountains in Europe were perceived as ugly and frightening in an early phase. In a second phase, leading up to the present, this negative image tipped towards its positive opposite. Recent research has relativised and clarified this traditional black-and-white periodisation. On the basis of many texts, it can be shown that the older mountain perception was of a mixed kind, positive or negative depending on the situation. What really changed in the transition to modernity were (1) the relative weight of these valuations, (2) their level of mandatoriness and (3) the frequency of perception. From the eighteenth century onwards, mountains received much more attention than before, the positive attributes gained weight over the negative ones and were subject to conventionalisation. It was now good manners to praise the mountains.[27]

Towards 1800, the mountain research begun by Scheuchzer and others expanded geographically, while Bible-based religion receded. Instead, a vocabulary from the borderlands of aesthetic and religious experience spread, with the leitmotif of the 'sublime'. An important pioneer and representative of this generation was the German naturalist Alexander von Humboldt (1769–1859). With his journey to South America, he made a great name for himself. In 1802, he even attempted to climb the over 6,000 metres high Chimborazo in present-day Ecuador, which had been considered the highest point on earth since the French meridian survey. When Humboldt later publicised the mountain with an illustrated book, he referred to the European readership's experience with well-known mountains and their appropriate description:

Travellers who have approached the summits of Mont Blanc and Mont Rose are alone capable of feeling the character of this calm, majestic, and solemn scenery. The bulk of Chimborazo is so enormous that the part which the eye embraces at once near the limit of the eternal snows is seven thousand metres in breadth. The extreme rarity of the strata of air, across which we see the tops of the Andes, contributes greatly to the splendour of the snow, and the magical effect of its reflection.[28]

Until the second half of the nineteenth century, many mountaineers stated that they wanted to contribute to research, like Humboldt. More and more, however, other motives came to the fore in the increasingly organised alpinism. The *Alpine Journal* of the English Alpine Club, for example, bore the subtitle *A Record of Mountain Adventure and Scientific Observation* from the first publication in 1863. Although preference was now given to adventure and experience and a competitive sport was pursued, in which a major aim was to achieve first ascents, the educational tradition with internal lecture series continued. In 1918, club member Hugh E.M. Stutfield chose the unusual lecture topic *Mountaineering as a Religion*. The fervour of mountaineers reminded him of true believers, and the distinction from non-mountaineers was sectarian in character. While mountaineering appears from the outside to be a pastime, the devotion to the mountains is in essence a religious reverence, even worship. The true alpinist defends his terrain against ordinary tourists as 'holy ground' to which only the demigods of ice axes and ropes have access.[29] A pastor from near London reacted enthusiastically to the depiction:

> The mountains have done the spiritual side of me more good religiously, as well as in my body physically, than anything else in the world. No one knows who and what God is until he has seen some real mountaineering and climbing in the Alps.[30]

In fact, climbers occasionally mentioned religious expressions to characterise the summit experience. Now and then, a prayer also occurred, which at least did not exclude nature.[31] Such statements and practices found more favour because, with the advent of scientific measurement, height above sea level had become the central criterion of interest. Sometimes the Greek Mount Olympus with its ancient world of gods was also mentioned. There were many educated citizens among alpinists, and the neo-humanism of the nineteenth century revitalised the classical tradition.[32] In the mouths of modern alpinists, however, talk of the Christian God or un-Christian gods often had a metaphorical or ironic character, as in Stutfield's lecture. The argument lacked the transcendental dimension that could hardly be claimed for sport (later, the comparison was often used for football).³³ Overall, the lecture seems to have said more about the speaker's changed concept of religion than about alpinism. In fact, he was working on a book about political-religious issues at the time and was looking for a new position.³⁴

While the British (and other) mountaineers in Europe came into contact with religious phenomena only sporadically, they were unmistakably confronted with them on the Indian subcontinent and in the Himalayas. Shortly after Stutfield's lecture, the first serious attempt was made to climb Mount Everest. This had replaced the earlier 'highest mountains' since the mid-nineteenth century and was now considered the ultimate goal of exploration and conquest alpinism. The corps that approached the mountain giant from Tibet in the spring of 1922 had thus an appropriate conquering appearance: it comprised a dozen British *sahibs* (gentlemen), including a filmmaker, accompanied by a translator, a military escort and numerous native porters, cooks and other auxiliaries, plus about 300 pack animals. On 30 April, the column led by a brigadier-general reached Rongbuk Monastery on the northern approach to Everest at over 5,000 metres. The monastery had only recently been founded and was considered strictly religious. Reluctantly, the abbot began to question the British leader about his intentions.

The general tried to present the expedition as a pilgrimage, which he called a white lie in a later report, and promised that they would not kill any animals there. Finally, the abbot gave his blessing and, according to his autobiography, admonished the expedition: 'As our country is bitterly cold and frosty, it is difficult for others than those devoted to religion not to come to harm. As the local spirits are furies, you must act with great firmness.' The British acted so, but the climb failed tragically, as did the next attempt two years later. In the meantime, eleven people had died. Tibet was a closed country; there were religious reservations against mountaineering. The British could obtain permission to climb Everest if Tibet again got into major disputes with China and was in need of support. Such an opportunity arose in 1930. The Dalai Lama now informed the British envoy that in his country almost every snow mountain was a seat of the gods and tutelary deities of the inner religion (Buddhism), which had to be regarded as 'very jealous'. For diplomatic reasons, however, he was prepared to put aside his reservations and grant permission.³⁵

From Theology to Religious Studies

In the East and West of Eurasia – to summarise this chapter – mountain-related beliefs and knowledge interacted in different ways. Chinese state-formation took place on a substrate of local mountain cults and led to an official hierarchy of sacred mountains. The older five imperial peaks were joined by the four Buddhist peaks by around 1600. Belief and knowledge about mountains covered the same territory and were closely intertwined.[36] In Europe, by contrast, mountains played a minor role in public perception. The Christian faith offered few points of reference. The most important impetus for increased attention came from natural history emerging in the early modern period. By referring to the religious discourse of nature as God's creation, research legitimised itself and at the same time brought about a certain religious valorisation of the environment. However, the secular measurement of mountains and their physical ascent and occupation remained dominant. While mountains in China were included in the governmental system and its hierarchy, in Europe they were classified according to their height. This resulted in a historical succession of 'highest mountains in the world': the Pico del Teide on Tenerife, often mentioned from the late Middle Ages, was followed in the mid-eighteenth century by the Chimborazo in Ecuador and in the mid-nineteenth century by Mount Everest in the Himalayas.[37]

Europe's imperialist expansion was associated with cultural confrontation and inspiration and led to a massive change in the perception of the environment. Knowledge was generally easier to transfer than belief, which was strongly context-bound and charged with feelings of identity. In Europe, the exposure to other forms of cult was one of the reasons for the emergence of a special science of religion, which established itself in the twentieth century alongside traditional theology. This opened up new possibilities for the mountain theme. It is worthwhile to conclude with a look at some of the actors in this development.

The empirical prelude was made by the geologist Ferdinand Freiherr von Andrian (1835–1914). He worked at the Austrian Geological Office and later became a commissioner for mining and forestry. His passion, however, was ethnology. In 1870 he founded the Anthropological Society in Vienna and twenty years later he published the book *The High Altitude Cultus of Asian and European Peoples* (*Der Höhencultus asiatischer und europäischer Völker*), which, at over 300 pages, remained the most detailed treatise on the subject for a long time.[38] Its aim was to investigate 'a widespread mountain worship' which 'emerges very clearly in the cults, literatures, myths and customs of the individual ethnic groups'. However, the unevenness of the distribution was as clear as its wide geographical range: the author had much more to offer on Asia than on Europe. The work resulted above all from the 'desire to collect', the general emergence of which pleased the author. He cited great names in philology, Indo-Germanic studies, classical studies and ethnology, from the Brothers Grimm to the linguist and religious scholar Max Müller and the anthropologist Edward Tylor. In terms of content, he subscribed, among other things, to the controversial thesis that Chinese culture was strongly influenced by Babylonian Mesopotamia.[39]

When (as in this case) new information combined with barely consolidated theses of the culture of knowledge, it was different from its encounters with firmly anchored ideas of the culture of faith. Theology was likewise exposed to the European collective lust for foreign texts and experiences, but it reacted to the renewal with far more restraint. Two pioneers of modern religious studies show how this transformation took place: Rudolf Otto and Mircea Eliade.

Rudolf Otto (1869–1937) was a professor of Protestant theology in Marburg with an interest in history, philosophy and non-Christian, especially Asian, religions. He was also familiar with these through travel. In 1911/12 he visited India, Burma, Japan and China.[40] Five years later, he published *The Idea of the Holy* (*Das Heilige*), a work that immediately made him famous. In it, he took human religious experience as his starting point and subjected it to a theological-philosophical interpretation. Thus, holiness was different from how it was defined by the Council of Trent (see Chapter 1). There, the official procedure for the church identification of the holy was determinative, whereas Otto conceived the phenomenon from the subjective perspective as a religious feeling with irrational moments (simultaneously terrifying and delightful). In some respects, this was a liberation from dogmatic precepts. However, the opening towards nature was kept within narrow limits. Only the emphasis on the 'sublime' in the context of the sacred and numinous could indicate an implicit reference to nature. Otto, however, explicitly attributed the veneration of environmental objects, including mountains, to archaic societies in history and the present. Christianity was clearly superior to these and ultimately remained unsurpassable.[41]

Forty years later, in 1957, a book was published entitled *The Sacred and the Profane*, which followed Otto in the preface, but took a different direction in terms of content. The Romanian-born author Mircea Eliade (1907–1986) had spent three years studying in India and later made a career as a religious scholar and writer in Paris and the United States. With this book, he wanted to summarise his knowledge and explain the essence of the religious. For the *homo religiosus*, primarily at home in archaic societies, everything is sacred, he wrote in many variations. Unlike Otto, who ultimately aimed at revitalising and affirming his community of believers, Eliade was dominated by these non-Christian experiences. Already in the first pages it becomes clear how much the reference to nature changes as a result. Modern occidental man finds it difficult to understand that the sacred can manifest itself in stones or trees. For many others, however, the whole of nature is a source of cosmic sacredness. Together with other elements, mountains are, according to Eliade, a symbol for the mythical centre of the cosmos, the *axis mundi* (world axis). Whether real or mythical, for him the peaks form a connection between heaven and earth in many cultures.[42]

Eliade has been heavily criticised in recent decades: overgeneralisation and lack of context and empirical evidence (for example regarding the implausible figure of *homo religiosus*) were repeatedly raised scientific objections.[43] But his work's archaeo-religiousness fell on fertile ground in the period of ecological awakening from the mid-1960s. Many forms of faith were themselves part of the awakening and were examined for their environmental compatibility and adapted under certain circumstances. *Greening of Religion* is the name given to the trend in the Anglo-Saxon area, whence it emanated above all.[44]

Edwin Bernbaum, an American mountaineer, religious scholar and environmental activist, was on a Peace Corps mission in Nepal at the time of this change. There, he came into contact with local religions and wrote his first book, which was followed by a dissertation at Berkeley in 1985. At that time, he was already working on his global work *Sacred Mountains of the World*, which was published in two editions in 1990 and 1997. One hundred years after Andrian's *High Altitude Cultus,* this opulently illustrated volume indicated in its presentation that the idea of a general sacredness of the mountains met with far more acceptance in the late twentieth century than previously. Displaying much knowledge and stylistic elegance, Bernbaum tried to strengthen this idea. In doing so, he sometimes called for an almost religious-like veneration of the mountains and even included them in his thanks ('And for the insight and joy they have given me, I would like to offer my gratitude to the mountains themselves').[45]

The fact that Bernbaum met with certain reservations in Christian regions was of little concern to him. When we invited him to a conference in Engelberg ('Mountain of Angels'), Switzerland, in 2007, he was delighted with the name – an obvious proof of his thesis. I had to disappoint him by specifying that there was no mountain called Engelberg, but merely a monastery and, starting from there, a human settlement, that is, in the traditional Christian manner of the saint. He was used to such discussions, for meanwhile he was designing a *Sacred Mountains Program* of environmental education for American national parks. He also often appeared at leadership events, including the World Economic Forum in Davos. When Mount Kailash in Tibet was to be nominated for UNESCO World Heritage, Bernbaum was the logical choice to lead the consultative negotiations.[46]

What Kailash, this 'mountain of all mountains' (Reinhold Messner's phrase), and its history look like on the ground provides the subject of the next chapter.

MOUNTAIN ITINERARIES

~ 3 ~

MOUNT KAILASH – MODEL MOUNTAIN OF HOLINESS

Mount Kailash is located in the Transhimalaya, in the sparsely populated west of Tibet, not far from the Indian and Nepalese borders. It has a symmetrical shape, converging like a pyramid at the top, is 6,638 metres high and lies in the area of tension between different traditions. This is also evident in its names: *Kailash* is Hindi, in Tibetan the peak is called *Tise* or *Gang Rinpoche* and there are also other names. A mythological guidebook from 1896, written by an important Tibetan monk, describes the appearance of the mountain as perceived by four groups, progressing from 'lower' to 'higher'. For non-Buddhists in the area, it is 'a glistening and lofty snow mountain rising into the sky like a king upon his throne. And it has so much magnificence because its minor peaks are arranged in the manner of ministers bowed before it.' For Hindus, Buddhists and initiated Buddhist Tantrics, the inner qualities count more than the outer appearance. The glory is due to the father-mother connection of the resident deities Shiva and Parvati (Hinduism) or the presence of the great Buddhist saint Angaja with his retinue of 500 blessed ones (Buddhism). It can also be conceived as a mandala of 62 deities at the centre of an enlightened palace, as in the story of the Grand Master Milarepa (Tantrism).[1]

In the years before 1900, at the time of this description, Mount Kailash was located in a peripheral part of a theocratic state closed off from the outside. It was known in Tibet as a high-ranking mountain, but was not visited very often and, even in India, was only noted by certain sections of the population in some areas. A hundred years later, its reputation had spread worldwide. Western literature in particular now praised it almost unanimously as the holiest mountain of all. How could this happen?

A Global Career

At the beginning of the nineteenth century, Tibet is said to have had 760,000 monks and nuns, twice as many as in the more populous Europe of the early modern period. It was a monastic state in whose history the Buddhist hierarchy and the monasteries played a major role. Like other regions of Central Asia, Tibet was exposed to imperialism from Britain (under the Indian viceroyalty), Russia and China. To forestall a feared Russian influence, the British undertook a bloody campaign to Lhasa in 1903/4. From then on, the southern border of the country was controlled by the colonial administration; for certain groups it was now more permeable than before. After the British withdrew from the subcontinent, the new Indian state took over this role and soon found itself facing communist China in the Himalayas. In 1950, Chinese troops invaded Tibet. In its revolutionary phase, the ruling party under Mao Zedong wanted to forcibly secularise the Buddhist highlands. Their leader, the fourteenth Dalai Lama, fled with many others to India, where he formed a government-in-exile. Tibet was closed again between about 1960 and 1980, after which the Chinese leadership took a different course.[2]

The seclusion and the two re-openings of this religious 'roof of the world' contributed not a little to the Western myth of Tibet. These events increased curiosity and, in a sense, satisfied it intermittently. Reports started early, but mentioned the holy Kailash only in passing. Even the first best-selling book by an adventure writer, *In the Forbidden Land* (1898), did not praise the mountain, but described it as unpleasantly angular and extremely unpicturesque.[3] After the British campaign, the coverage increased and changed. In the book *Western Tibet and the British Borderlands* (1906), Kailash appeared in a better light, including its shape. Written by a colonial official with an interest in the development of the borderlands, the text emphasised the important role of the region in religious thought: Mount Kailash was 'the Heaven of Buddhists and Hindus, answering to the Olympus of Homer'. At present, the author remarked, the mountain was visited by a few hundred pilgrims a year but, with improved transport routes, there could soon be thousands. The frontispiece was adorned with a photograph of the mountain; in many chapters, the inspection and travel report dealt with religious topics.[4]

The two English books were republished several times, but not translated. The writings of the Swedish Central Asian explorer Sven Hedin (1865–1952) found a much larger, international readership. They appeared in numerous languages, including Chinese and Japanese. In his two-volume work *Trans-Himalaya. Discoveries and Adventures in Tibet* (1909), the successful author described how he undertook the religious circumambulation ritual of Mount Kailash as a 'heathen' on horseback, while his native companions walked on foot: 'they are Lamaists, and are glad of the opportunity to come nearer the

Figure 5. The holy Kailash behind Lake Manasarovar on the cover of Sven Hedin's Transhimalaja, 1912 (German edition).

gates of salvation by wandering round the holy mountain'.[5] The mountain now became tangible around the globe in text and image. As with Hedin's other expeditions, however, the Tibet trip was primarily about questions of Western science, presented in a popular way with adventures and anecdotes. The focus was on mapping and locating the sources of the great Indian rivers. Hedin's research was made possible thanks to his connections to the highest state circles, which further consolidated the fame of the author and his writings. As a result of his unconditional partisanship for Germany in the First World War and his later relationship with Adolf Hitler, however, his reputation took on a clear political tinge.[6]

In the interwar period, popular travel and adventure literature on the Himalayas increasingly used religious titles. A book published in 1937 by a geologist and youthful adventurer from Austria, which also advertised itself with a foreword by Hedin, was called *To the Holiest Mountain in the World* (*Zum heiligsten Berg der Welt*). A year later, two Swiss geoscientists gave their expedition report the title *Throne of the Gods* (*Thron der Götter*). The religious veneration of Kailash was only one topic among many, and the statements oscillated between admiration and condescension. The authors disguised themselves as local pilgrims, keeping their geologist's hammers and other instruments hidden. It was known that rock surveys could cause irritation among believers.[7]

From the growing body of literature on Kailash, one more work should be mentioned that did not just use religion as an exotic advertising medium, but made it its core and concern: *The Way of the White Clouds* by the German cultural scholar and artist Ernst Lothar Hoffmann, who converted to Buddhism and became known as Lama Anagarika Govinda (1898–1985). It was a spiritual autobiography based on a journey to Tibet shortly before the Chinese invasion. By the time the book was published in several languages in the late 1960s, the highlands had once again been closed. At the same time, interest in the region increased in the West with the youth revolt and the expanded political-cultural search for meaning. To date, the work has gone through dozens of editions, making it arguably the Kailash bestseller with the widest reach.[8] I will come back to this work later in this chapter.

All in all, the interest in Kailash experienced a steep ascent. Around 1935, two works on the new field of mountain geography appeared independently of each other, which both spoke about sacred mountains without mentioning Kailash. By the end of the century, the situation was quite different: around 1990, the relevant surveys unanimously presented the difficult-to-access mountain in this high border region as the holiest mountain on the planet.[9] The idea of a global holiness ranking is not self-evident. It may have been influenced by the alpinist struggle to conquer the highest mountain. In any case, Everest was mentioned in this context as early as the 1930s, and in recent decades Kailash has been presented as a spiritual antithesis, so to speak: not as high as, but holier than Mount Everest. The main argument for this judgement was the multicultural aura of Mount Kailash. It has enjoyed a high status in four religions since time immemorial: Hinduism, Buddhism, Jainism and Bön. Thus, the number of devotees could be estimated at many hundreds of millions.[10]

Tantra, Demchock and Shiva

On closer inspection, this estimate proves to be artificial and misleading. In reality, the 'religions' mentioned consisted of diverse traditions and did not have unified dogmas adhered to by all believers. The historian Alex McKay, who has recently presented a critical overall account (on which we can largely rely here), therefore examines various *histories* which, in his eyes, cannot be combined into a Kailash story that comes from a single mould. He also warns against exaggerated expectations regarding the tradition's antiquity.[11]

Tibetan Buddhism had its historical roots in India and is still oriented towards this 'holy land of the Buddha'. In both areas, religious renunciation of the world and the master–disciple relationship play a major role within and outside Buddhism. The practitioners of the emerging tradition of a specialised, often mobile, eremitic and ascetic search for God bore many names (yogis, fakirs, sadhus, etc.). The tantras, a genre of texts widespread since the second half of the first millennium, became very important. McKay describes them thus:

> Central to this category was the developed understanding that the individual could become their chosen deity, or at least acquire the powers of that deity. Tantra was a means to achieve this state through self-identification with the deity by a highly ritualised series of practices potentially applicable to any deity.[12]

Regardless of religious affiliation, this esoteric doctrine, accessible only to initiates, had a strong influence on the spiritual life of the subcontinent and the Himalayas.

The discovery of Kailash as a Tantric means of meditation and identification mainly occurred in the early thirteenth century, when 'treasures' of other highly sacred mountains, such as Tsari in south-eastern Tibet, were also 'opened' (see Chapter 1). It is very doubtful in the case of Kailash whether the opening was preceded by a local, collective mountain cult of lay people. The pioneering role probably lay entirely with immigrating hermits. Together with

Mount Kailash – Model Mountain of Holiness

Mount Kailash, the adjacent Lake Manasarovar to the south was, and still is, worshipped. The mountain–water complex gained sacredness through the reputation of successive religious masters. The visit in 1616 of the Panchen Lama, a high dignitary from an important reincarnation lineage, promoted all-Tibetan recognition. As a result of a bitter political conflict, the suzerainty over a number of monasteries from the region was donated to faraway Bhutan 60 years later; the most important of these monasteries was Darchen, at the starting point of the circumambulation route. By the nineteenth century, the attribution of significance to the state had reached the point where Kailash could be invoked and attested as a witness in a border treaty.[13]

In Tibetan, the main Kailash deity is called Demchock, described in ancient Tantric texts as a very powerful deity whose mandala scheme usually includes 62 auxiliary deities. The most famous master of this lineage is the poet and saint Milarepa. He is said to have won Kailash for Buddhism in a magical battle with a rival. Like the tantras, the circumambulation ritual originated in India, where sacred objects were worshipped in this form across denominations. As far as I can see, the circumambulation of mountains is not practised elsewhere in the world. And even in Tibet and the surrounding area, it was mostly limited to a number of highly sacred mountains.[14]

For the laity, it gave a measure of the sin-redeeming power of the pilgrimage. At Tsari, which was the most important mountain shrine for the Buddhist elite in Lhasa until the twentieth century (see Chapter 1), participation in a 'great ravine circuit' seems to have atoned even for the cardinal sin of murder. At Kailash, it took thirteen circuits for an unintentional kill. Those who had circled the mountain thirteen times by the normal route (a good 50 kilometres at an altitude of 4,575 to 5,640 metres) were also authorised to choose the short, inner route close to the summit for subsequent rounds. Pilgrims could increase the level of religious commitment by constantly prostrating themselves and getting up again. This meant that a circumambulation on the normal route took several weeks instead of two or three days. Buddhists justified the practice, which was criticised by Western visitors, by saying that it significantly intensified physical contact with the holy ground.[15]

Indian Kailash worship had partly different origins, and its symbolic figure became Shiva, a Hindu chief god who resided on the peak with his wife Parvati. The classical religious epics and legends (*Mahabharata*, *Ramayana*, *Puranas*), however, only spoke of the sacred character of the Himalayas as a mountain massif. If the name of a single peak was mentioned, it was the mythical Mount Meru (or Sumeru), and if the name Kailash (or Kailasa) really appeared in the text, the localisation remained uncertain. In northern India there are a number of mountains with this name. Moreover, according to the epic scriptures, Shiva had numerous residences throughout the country.[16] That the imaginary geography does not coincide with the factual geography, but has a momentum of its own, is not uncommon with mountains – sacred or not. In this case, however, the difference seems to have been particularly great. Nevertheless, Tibetan Kailash became a sanctuary associated with Shiva for itinerant religious specialists from India and later for ordinary pilgrims. As we have seen above, in the early twentieth century this amounted to a few hundred people a year. British colonial officials promoted pilgrimage because they hoped it would bring regional economic growth and increase their influence in Tibet.

Buddhism for All

The opening of the border also let into the country mountaineers who aspired to Alpine ventures, which seemed very questionable from a religious point of view because the peaks here belonged to the deities. The resulting conflict led to a trial of strength that was first fought out on the spot and later negotiated in an extended public sphere. The aforementioned *To the Holiest Mountain in the World* (1937) faked a conversation in which a local answered the 'unwise question' of whether the 'throne of the gods' would one day be conquered by Europeans. No one was capable of climbing Kailash, he said, unless that person had never committed a sin and could transform himself into a bird to fly over the steep ice walls to the summit.[17] Swami Pranavananda, an Indian author who combined a modernised Hinduism with Western science, wanted in a 1949 publication to promote secular tourism in the Kailash region in addition to pilgrimage. He apparently considered the idea of sea-planes on the holy Lake Manasarovar unproblematic. Summit ascents seemed less realistic to him. It remained uncertain whether and when such an undertaking would be approved by the 'conservative, superstitious, and suspicious Tibetans'.[18] After the second opening of the country, rumours of planned ascents circulated several times; to this day, however, religious respect seems to have remained dominant and the summit has not been reached.

Pranavananda's writing also points to the changing of religious ideas in the modern context. This is very clear in *The Way of the White Clouds* by Anagarika Govinda, a German convert to Buddhism who had lived on the Indian subcontinent since 1928 and immersed himself in the religious traditions. The book was written in the early 1960s, when he became a focal point for spiritually interested exponents of the American counterculture and set off on his lecture tours, which took him to several continents. The preface begins with a brilliant critique of progress and invites the reader to follow the author on a pilgrimage through his life and to Kailash (he visited it in 1948, sponsored by the *Illustrated Weekly of India*) under the symbol of white clouds, as seen in Buddhist paintings.[19]

In Govinda's text, Kailash became a vessel of cosmic forces. What is important about mountains, he said, is not their height, but their spiritual greatness. 'Mountains grow and decay, they breathe and pulsate with life. They attract and collect invisible energies from their surroundings', namely from air, water, electricity and magnetism. But even among great mountains, there are only a few that are so outstanding that they become symbols of the highest aspirations of humanity, 'milestones of the eternal quest for perfection and ultimate realisation, signposts that point beyond our earthly concerns towards the infinity of a universe from which we have originated and to which we belong'. Although only a select group of people could free themselves from the daily pursuit of money and pleasures, together they formed a constant stream of pilgrims. 'Thus it is that above all the sacred mountains of the world the fame of Kailash has spread and inspired human beings since times immemorial.'[20]

It was a message for Buddhist-inspired followers of various religions and also simply for the spiritually interested. After the hardships of the arduous pilgrimage, the new visitors could hope for moments of supreme bliss, ecstasy and trance-like states, which the author claimed to have experienced. In the rest of the book, he adeptly defended Tibetan Buddhism against Western critics who, since the nineteenth century, had mainly targeted demon fear, sectarian rivalry and certain magical and monastic practices. He considered himself a reincarnation of the German poet Novalis.[21]

Subsequently, the defence of Tibet and its symbol of sanctity also passed into Western hands. The shift was clearly expressed when the Chinese authorities wanted to turn the pilgrimage route around Mount Kailash into a road in 2003. The authorities claimed that the road would benefit pilgrims making the circumambulations. The Tibetan government-in-exile in India was of the same opinion this time, but warned against abusing the holy mountain as a tourist destination. The Tibet Initiative Germany saw this as a colonial act that only served commercial development for the Chinese and trampled on the religious sensibilities of Tibetans, as well as 800 million Hindus in India. The association appealed to the German government, the European Union and the Indian government to oppose the project. Supported by partners from other European countries and the German Alpine Club, the Tibet Initiative organised a Kailash demonstration on the Zugspitze, Germany's highest mountain.[22]

At the time of this protest, a third of the approximately 20,000 people who now visited Kailash in ordinary years were already described as tourists and not pilgrims. Many of them were from India and the West.[23] The extent to which the remote mountain had entered the Western-dominated global culture is shown by the fact that its designation turned into a label when needed. Around 2010, a young music group in Germany was asked why they had adopted the name Kailash: 'Because it is a spiritual symbol joining peace and harmony with the whole world, a symbol originating from Asia, where the spirit culture still gains on the materialism,' was the answer.[24] The complex, ambiguous and sometimes problematic history of the mountain had dissolved into a hopeful message.

~ 4 ~

TAI SHAN – THE IMPERIAL EASTERN MOUNTAIN

Tai Shan is located in the Chinese province of Shandong, scarcely 500 kilometres south of Beijing. It is a medium mountain massif that stands out clearly from the densely populated, low-lying plains and rises to 1,545 metres. Tai Shan is the most prominent of the *Wuyue*, the country's 'Five Great Mountains' (see Chapter 2), and looks back on a very old religious and political history. This is also visible on the surface of the mountain, which is littered with buildings in many places. A nine-kilometre-long stone staircase connects the starting point on the plain with the 'Southern Gate of Heaven', a tower-like passage on the mountain ridge. There, the pilgrimage route turns east and reaches its highest point at the 'Peak of the Jade Emperor'. The ascent is strenuous and takes time; four to six hours is quoted. Until the twentieth century, Chinese dignitaries and scholars had themselves carried up with special palanquins. Since 1983, it has also been possible to reach the summit by aerial cableway.[1]

After this technical innovation, a closed China under the rule of the Communist Party also wanted to gain access to the Western world and applied to UNESCO for Tai Shan to be included in the World Heritage List. It was now considered a national symbol, just like the Great Wall and several other sites for which applications were also made. UNESCO, the United Nations cultural organisation headquartered in Paris, had begun registering cultural and natural properties of 'inestimable value to all mankind' and placing them under special protection in the 1970s. This required examination by experts. The International Union for Conservation of Nature (IUCN) was only moderately convinced by the geology, flora and other environmental qualities of Tai Shan and criticised the management and tourist development of the much-visited mountain. However, IUCN considered it an impressive cultural phenomenon existing only because of the mountain's natural characteristics. It consisted of monuments, ancient architectural complexes, stone sculptures and archaeological sites of extraordinary importance: 'There are 22 temples, 97 ruins, 819 stone tablets and 1,018 cliffside and stone inscriptions.'[2]

Landscape as a History Book

In December 1987, Tai Shan was accepted by UNESCO. China had promised to comply with certain requests for changes and to improve management. Like much else, this event soon found a stone signature on the mountain. Immediately next to earlier imperial inscriptions, Li Ping, Premier and Chairman of the State Council of the People's Republic of China, had the inscription carved into the rock in stylish, large-format calligraphy: 'Protect the world's heritage and establish the Eastern Sacred Peak'.[3]

Landscape as a History Book

Even at the beginning of the modern era, there was no shortage of rock inscriptions. Those who had made their way to the top in the sixteenth century and were able to read could take note of an almost 800-year-old message from the Tang dynasty under the summit – 17 metres high, with 16-centimetre characters inlaid with gold pigment: 'I have occupied the imperial rank for fourteen years, yet I am not virtuous and I am ignorant of the perfect Way', proclaimed Emperor Xuanzong (reigned 712–756). He had discussed with many officials whether it was right to make the great sacrifice to heaven, before, accompanied by the army, he finally set out and performed it on top of Tai Shan. 'Truly, it is the grandson of the Heavenly Lord, the dwelling of the assembled spirits. Its location is the origin of all things, and thus it is called Dai. Its position is that of the elder of the Five Marchmounts, and therefore it is called "ancestor".' Heaven gives birth to the multitude of the people, the emperor continued, but only the ruler has to rule. If he fulfilled Heaven's mandate in an exemplary manner, all could live in abundance, enriched by the blessings of the spirits. 'I therefore have polished a stone wall and carved this golden record, so that later men hearing my words will know my heart.'[4]

In the sixteenth century, the rise of the great pilgrimage to Tai Shan accelerated. In parallel, the inscription of the landscape increased. When the Emperor Kangxi (reigned 1661–1722) visited the mountain in the late seventeenth century, he had 'Cloudy Peak' (Yunfeng) carved into the rock with two striking characters. According to him, they were to illuminate the famous mountain and share eternity with Tai Shan. His grandson, Emperor Qianlong (reigned 1736–1795), visited the peak six times. Underneath his grandfather's two characters, he placed wordy poems, and at another spot he had his verses carved into a steep face across an area of twenty by nine metres. These were only the writings from the highest hands. Officials and scholars also took part in the affixing of such *moya* signs, which is the Chinese term for mountain inscriptions. Occasionally, this involved deliberate overwriting or commenting on earlier utterances. Robert E. Harrist, an expert in this field, points out that the culture of inscribing nature, which goes back to the beginning of the Common Era, was an especially Chinese preference. The inscriptions of the Roman Empire, for example, are found mainly on buildings and rarely on bare rock.[5]

Figure 6. Rock inscriptions on the summit of Tai Shan, 2007.

Tai Shan was not only the place to communicate with heaven and the immortals. He was also a god himself, endowed with titles by the emperor and supplicated with prayers. From the Tang dynasty to the end of the Middle Ages, the god had been promoted several times: *Heavenly King* (726 CE), *Good, Holy, Heavenly King* (1008), *Good, Holy, Heavenly Emperor* (1011), *Heavenly Emperor, Great Bringer of Life, Good and Holy* (1291). Eighty years later, the title inflation ended and it was declared that no human designation could match the qualities of the sacred mountain, so henceforth it was simply called *Eastern Peak Tai Shan*.[6] This is how it then appeared in the early modern prayers that the emperors issued from their courtly residence in the form of stone steles to be erected in the mountain temples when the occasion arose: in the case of a drought that endangered the transport of grain on the canals in 1510; in the case of floods and the machinations of rebels and brigands in 1511; when the emperor had no son and heir in 1532; in thanksgiving for the birth of a male heir to the throne in 1538, and so on.[7]

The Rise of the Goddess

The Tai Shan God also had temples, especially a large complex at the foot of the mountain and the starting point for pilgrimage. The annual state rituals were held there by imperial officials and the accommodation and entertainment industry was concentrated there. Its religious veneration also spread over large parts of the empire. In numerous towns and villages, people did not want to be inferior to the central complex, and built their own temples in which characters referred to the supernatural abilities of Tai Shan (such as 'His godly power rewards and punishes'; 'To escape His deep sight is difficult').[8]

Another pillar of the ruling culture was Confucius, the Chinese sage and teacher par excellence, who is dated to the middle of the first millennium BCE. Tales of his experiences and statements on Tai Shan had long circulated, but he did not receive his own buildings there until modern times: a gate at the foot of the mountain to mark the beginning of his ascent, built in 1560, and a temple near the summit, erected around 1583; other sites were declared his vantage points and furnished with pavilions. Scholars and men of letters were thus able to walk in the footsteps of their role model.[9] The question of whether Confucianism represents an (ancestor-oriented) religion or an (at times hotly debated) philosophical-moral tradition remains controversial in the literature. The multi-faceted veneration that the master enjoyed at Tai Shan indicates that both views have their plausibility. From incense offerings and nature contemplation to historical tourism, there was much to choose from.[10] More surprising, however, is the fact that Chinese women were also able to get involved with a goddess on this mountain so full of masculine connotations.

The Rise of the Goddess

This goddess of Tai Shan, named Bixia Yuanjun, became the main goal of pilgrimage from the late Middle Ages. Thanks to her growing appeal, the general population also took part, causing the number of annual visits to reach at least 400,000. The numbers fluctuated considerably, but the order of magnitude can be estimated on the basis of the imperial pilgrimage tax introduced in 1516. The proportion of women is less certain. Estimates are based on inadequate sources and vary widely. Brian R. Dott has examined the stone stelae at Tai Shan on which organised pilgrimage groups were inscribed with date and name. There were gender-separated as well as mixed groups. On several dozen stelae from the seventeenth to the early twentieth centuries, the historian has found a total of a third were women, and assumes that this figure underestimates rather than overestimates female participation.[11]

Tai Shan – The Imperial Eastern Mountain

The main temple of Bixia Yuanjun on Tai Shan peak, which was renovated several times, was the largest religious institution on the holy mountain. The pilgrims hoped for and asked the goddess for family fertility, especially male offspring, as well as general wellbeing for body and life. Bixia covered a broad spectrum of female identity, which was vividly demonstrated by her titles: *Heavenly Immortal Jade Maiden* (Tianxian Yunü), *Holy Mother* (Shengmu) or *Old Grandmother* (Lao Nainai). The main hall of her temple was closed off with a lattice wall behind which stood the richly decorated statue of the goddess, flanked by auxiliary goddesses. Under the supervision of the resident Taoist monks and nuns, visitors could throw their offerings through the lattice at the feet of the sacred statues. As in many sacrificial rituals, incense was also lit in bronze vessels in the temple courtyard. The fragrant air contributed greatly to the religious atmosphere. 'Going on pilgrimage' was succinctly rendered in Chinese with two expressions: 'paying respect to the mountain' (*ch'ao-shan*) and 'offering incense' (*chin-hsiang*).[12]

In 1608, an author noted that all the inhabitants from areas north of the Yangtze River would make a pilgrimage to the 'Great Mountain' to offer incense. In doing so, the ordinary people would behave properly at the beginning and observe many things: the vegetarian rules and other taboos, proper dress and feelings of respect. But as soon as the prayers and ceremonies were over, they would indulge in debauched festivities. In fact, the pilgrimage to Tai Shan covered a catchment area of about 300 to 350 kilometres. Despite modest demands and favourable overall offers, it often required considerable outlay. By forming pilgrimage groups with joint funds and the possibility to pay over a longer period of time, these costs could be met.[13] Even greater than the catchment area was the reputational aura of Tai Shan. In addition to the male cult with the temples mentioned above, the female Bixia cult also spread over a wide area. During the early modern period, the goddess of Tai Shan became one of the most important female deities in northern China. She was present in various media, from fictional literature to 'spirit money': cheap block prints that could be pinned to the wall at home and later burned as offerings.[14]

State officials and Confucian scholars were suspicious of popular Bixia worship. It was considered licentious and unnecessary, if not dangerous. The dubious rituals, the unacceptable forms of miracles and the excessive passion, which could even lead to ritual suicide, were criticised. Modern studies emphasise that the concerns raised also reflected the social struggle over the recognised roles of women and female sexuality.[15] In our context, the dogmatic discussion that took place at the imperial court is of interest. As early as 1516, the Ministry of Rites expressed doubts about the authenticity of the goddess. Ritual officials pointed out that there was no written evidence for her worship in classical antiquity. Nor could it be proven that she was a deified person who had lived in the period that followed. And if Bixia were the mountain spirit herself, she would have had to be worshipped in a different form and only by officials. However, the arguments do not seem to have caught on. Despite dubious status, the goddess continued to be protected, and one vocal critic soon fell victim to an alliance of powerful eunuchs. But the question continued to smoulder. Strict Confucians came back to it when the occasion arose. By contrast, the male god of Tai Shan, far less popular locally, had a firm foothold in the imperial ritual code.[16]

From Revolution to World Heritage

In the nineteenth century, the empire's traditionally dominant position in East Asia deteriorated. The population had increased significantly and the economy had intensified and diversified. But Western power politics, foreign ideas and scientific doctrines were causing problems for the ruling Qing dynasty. It had conquered China from Manchuria in the seventeenth century and taken over many institutions, including the nationwide imperial examination system for civil servants, which focused on cultural and literary competence and was designed for continuity in a Sinocentric world. Faced with the imperialist challenge, more and more intellectuals became convinced that profound change was inevitable. In the years after 1900, the imperial house also intervened, abolishing civil service examinations and attempting to build a new education system. Even before that, staunch supporters of reform had proclaimed that temples should be transformed into schools, which would also combat popular superstition.[17]

The conversion or destruction of temples built primarily of wood had a tradition in the empire and was perceived as less of a culture war than one might assume. Unlike in Christianity, where places of worship were liturgically consecrated, the sacred in China was concentrated in ritual objects, especially the statues of the deities and the incense burners. They could be transferred to another place if a temple fell out of favour. This had happened on several occasions, for example when a cult was deemed immoral by officials, or on the occasion of Confucian interventions against a Buddhist trend. In the twentieth century, however, it was no longer about different claims to power in a pluralistic religious system, but about the system as a whole. It is estimated that there were about one million temples in China at the beginning of the century; by the 1980s, the vast majority no longer seem to have existed.[18]

Tai Shan – The Imperial Eastern Mountain

The most important factors in this change were the revolutions and repeated campaigns for a new order. At the beginning of 1912, the new Chinese Republic overthrew the imperial house. Shortly afterwards, the Kuomingtang Party emerged, which later became embroiled in a triangular conflict (defence against Japan, alliance with and then hostility to Mao Zedong's Communist Party). In 1928, the Kuomingtang issued *Standards for Retaining or Abolishing Gods and Shrines*, saying:

> Superstition is an obstacle to progress, and the power of the gods is a way of keeping the people ignorant. Despite China's ancient civilization, because education is not yet spread widely, the poison of superstition is deeply embedded in the people's heart.

After the Communist Party finally took power and proclaimed the People's Republic of China in 1949, motives against traditional forms of religion multiplied. With its Marxist orientation, the party was officially committed to atheism. Temple property was systematically confiscated, and the early phase of the Cultural Revolution between about 1966 and 1968 saw a rigorously anti-traditional mass movement.[19] How did these turbulent times play out at Tai Shan?

The reformers and revolutionaries faced a certain dilemma here, as they wanted to play down the religious reputation of the holy mountain while maintaining and promoting the national reputation. Under Western pressure, the country was on its way to becoming a modern nation state and in need of symbols. In 1934, an author compared China's great river and mountain (Huang He, Tai Shan) to corresponding natural monuments in modern states like Germany (Rhine) and Japan (Fujiyama). At that time, many archways on the pilgrimage stairway of Tai Shan had already been painted over with the republican blue. The buildings were emblazoned with a picture of the revolutionary leader Sun Yat-sen, together with his political slogans. In addition, signs of technical modernity were added to the mountain in the form of a weather station. In the feverish atmosphere of the Cultural Revolution, plans were made to replace the temple of the Jade Emperor on the summit with a fifteen-metre-high statue of Mao. However, it ended up with a portrait on the Southern Gate of Heaven and a poem carved into the rock about the Long March of 1935, which the Chairman had written at the time and later copied onto a paper scroll in calligraphy.[20]

In 1965, the resident monks and nuns were forced to leave the temples on Tai Shan. For a time, general visitation was also severely restricted. The buildings seem to have been damaged mainly by neglect. It took a reorientation of Chinese national policy to give the mountain a function again. When the opening of the country and liberalisation began in the early 1980s, there was a sudden rush to renewed modernity. In 1983, the gondola lift to the summit was built. In 1985, religious staff returned (only to the Bixia temple and now with state-supervised training). By 1990, there were already three million visits per annum, far exceeding earlier figures, and later the number seems to have doubled again. There is no doubt that the veneration of the mountain underwent a strong secularisation in the course of the upheavals of the twentieth century. But just as veneration was not exclusively religious in imperial times, it did not become exclusively touristic in the recent past.[21]

In May 1987, the International Union for Conservation of Nature was to pass judgement on the inclusion of the Tai Shan in the UNESCO World Heritage List. Their conviction, as we saw at the beginning, was limited. The organisation was also not responsible for the cultural side of the professional judgement, which had to be decided by another agency. But it consoled itself with the statement that the many sediments of Chinese culture that had been deposited here 'exist only because of the natural characteristic of the mountain'.[22] This was a bold claim – given that the country had thousands of mountains but only one Tai Shan. Subsequently, UNESCO was to undergo an unprecedented learning process about the region. By 2020, over twenty Chinese mountains and mountain landscapes had been added to the World Heritage List and ascribed 'outstanding value of humanity' – far more than for any other country in the world. Since 2008, the entire imperial system of the Five Mountains, of which the Tai Shan was the head, has also been on the candidate list. The proposal was submitted by the Ministry of Construction of the People's Republic.[23]

In contrast, there is uncertainty about the UNESCO candidacy of the sacred Kailash in Tibet, which captivates people around the globe (see Chapter 3). In February 2015, an international environment and development centre in Kathmandu launched the Kailash Sacred Landscape Conservation and Development Initiative with the aim of submitting a transboundary Nepalese-Indian-Chinese application and thus also promoting biodiversity and other ecological concerns. But problems soon arose that were difficult to solve. The borders in the Himalayas are disputed, and it seems unlikely that the People's Republic of China would particularly promote a mountain on its territory that has also become a national symbol of Tibet.[24]

~ 5 ~

PAEKTUSAN – SACRED MOUNTAIN OF THE REVOLUTION

Paektusan or Mount Paektu is considered the most prominent mountain on the Korean peninsula. It is a remote, 2,744-metre-high volcano in the far north, in the sparsely populated area bordering Chinese Manchuria. A massive eruption in the tenth century left a huge crater at the top, where a lake formed over time. The volcano has erupted several times since then and is still considered active. Today, the border between North Korea and China runs through the middle of the picturesque body of water, in which the peaks of the crater rim and the wide sky are reflected. The mountain mainly gained its importance since the seventeenth century, through the search for historical-religious origins and against the background of increasing interstate power politics. On the Chinese side, Manchuria played a special role; on the Korean side, Japanese imperialism in the twentieth century and, subsequently, the division of the country into a capitalist South and a communist North provided the political framework.

The north has an unambiguous reputation today. The state is considered an inhumane dictatorship. It is hermetically sealed and subject to a persistent regime of international sanctions. Because so little information crosses the border and the image is so fixed, we have difficulty forming a differentiated picture of North Korea. When Kim Jong-il, the son of North Korean state founder Kim Il-sung, died in December 2011, a Swiss newspaper wrote: 'North Korea's state-run news agency, the Korean Central News Agency (KCNA), is abuzz with bizarre reports of the "Beloved Leader's" death. After heart-breaking images of mourning North Koreans, it now turns its attention to nature.' According to the agency, miracles were observed that prove that nature was also mourning the leader: cracked glaciers, mountains lighting up, cranes crouching in front of a statue of the deceased.[1] In the following, we will try to look behind such unusual images. We start with the Chinese side, since China was the dominant force in this area for centuries.

The Ancestors of the Manchus

The Chinese name for Paektusan is Changbaishan and refers to both the volcano with the crater lake and the larger mountain range. Other names have also been handed down in the historical writings of the empire. Mountain legends and cults seem to have been widespread in the region, but only came prominently to light in documented history in the seventeenth century, when Manchurian warlords succeeded in establishing themselves as rulers in the Chinese heartland and founded the new Qing dynasty.[2] After ascending the throne, they were keen to emphasise the role of the Manchus and especially their own ancestors vis-à-vis the Han Chinese. In 1677, Emperor Kangxi sent an expedition to Changbaishan. After several weeks of travel, the scouts stood at the densely forested foot of the mountain in mid-July:

> When we walked out of the woods, the mountains were shrouded in fog and clouds and we could not see anything. We knelt down before the mountain and chanted a prayer. The moment we were done, the fog cleared and the Changbai Mountains leapt up vividly before us. We were thunderstruck.[3]

At the top, the group explored the shape and dimensions of the summit region with its green, exceptionally pure lake. On the descent, a portentous event occurred. When the group came across a pack of deer, seven animals did not take flight like the others, but fell to the ground and rolled down the slope at the feet of the hungry men. They thought it was a gift from the 'mountain spirit' (*shanling*) and grabbed it. 'We accepted the deer and bowed to the mountain again.' At court in Beijing, Emperor Kangxi was pleased with the report. Evidently, he said, there were numerous miracles at this venerable place of origin, which his dynasty had received from the gods. He decreed that Changbaishan should be given an official title and regular sacrifices. The Ministry of Rites proposed semi-annual offerings to the mountain spirit. The emperor gave his consent, but added the significant clause that Changbaishan should be elevated to the level of the Five Sacred Mountains of China (*Wuyue*) and worshipped according to the same protocol.[4]

The expedition had not least been a fact-finding mission. The emperor had also justified it by saying that no one knew the exact place of origin of the Manchus in the area. A somewhat older 'true account' of their beginnings spoke of another mountain and mountain lake. There, heaven had sent down three immortal virgins for a bath. After refreshment, the youngest had eaten a red fruit brought by a bird. When the fruit swelled in her mouth, the virgin felt very pregnant and knew that – unlike her sisters – she could no longer return to heaven. She then gave birth to the progenitor of the Manchu clan (Aisin Gioro), who was born already able to speak.[5]

Through the expedition, Emperor Kangxi knew about Manchu geography, and later he began his large-scale empirical mapping work in the area. But his concern went further: he also wanted to map Chaibashan with geomantic methods and connect it to the Chinese heartland. The masters of geomancy (*fengshui*) paid attention to ground elevations in which positive energy was concentrated. The hills or mountains in question were called 'dragons' or 'veins of dragons'. Kangxi wrote a treatise entitled *Mount Tai's Mountain Veins Originate in the Changbai Mountains*. According to his own account, the emperor discovered this connection over a distance of more than 1,100 kilometres – about a third across the Yellow Sea – thanks to careful examination of terrain and geographical relations, including at sea. He explained in detail how the mountain ranges between his Manchu ancestral mountain and the most important Chinese imperial mountain ran. At the water's edge, the 'dragons' submerged for a while and raised their heads again on the other shore. Thus, the hierarchy of the mountains corresponded to the new balance of power. 'Although the ancients did not reach the conclusions of this essay, the topography truly proves them.'[6]

In the eighteenth century, a Romantic school of poetry and literature developed around Changbaishan, but few seem to have actually visited the remote mountain.[7] A similar story soon played out on the Korean side. The royal Joseon dynasty had been culturally and politically dependent on China since it came to power in the late fourteenth century, and it had its own system of sacred mountains. The dynasty seems to have fought its first battle for ascent to the throne in the north as well. The area was considered the northern gateway to the country and the 'place where the king arose'. But the Changbaishan, here called Paektusan, long played a subordinate role in the ritual order. At times, in scholarly discussions, it was even considered not to belong to the land. This changed in the middle of the eighteenth century, when the Manchu dynasty promoted it and the geography was better known. In 1761, the Korean court again wanted to determine the important peaks of the kingdom. For dynastic and topographical reasons, the head of the Ministry of Rites proposed that Paektusan should be the northern peak: 'There are no rivers or mountains that do not originate from Paektusan. This mountain is surely the origin of our country.' After several years of back and forth between the ruler and his officials, the proposal was decided. Paektusan was also given an official title in Korea and regular offerings.[8]

Korea's Progenitor

Around 1277, a Buddhist monk in Korea put down on paper an oral tale that initially attracted little attention but later became very significant. It tells of the deity Hwanung, who once descended from heaven to a mountain (usually identified as Paektusan), together with 3,000 spirits. Thanks to pious observance, a female bear turned into a human woman who was seeking a husband. Hwanung answered the prayer and begat Tangun with her. Tangun founded the first Korean state and lived from then on as a mountain god. His act took place at the time of the legendary Chinese emperor Yao. Later scholars set it to the year 2333 BCE.[9] In addition to this story, other founding narratives circulated from the sixteenth to the eighteenth century, including one that spoke of a land enfeoffment by the Chinese 'Son of Heaven'. This version was popular with Korean scholars, who drew on the prestigious culture of the Middle Kingdom, while the Tangun story was autonomist in character. According to research, it was not by chance that it was recorded during the oppressive Mongol rule.[10]

Mountain journeys were as popular with Confucian scholars and literati in Korea as with those in China. They often led to the mountains of the south and the central part of the country, which were dotted with Buddhist monasteries in places. Paektusan, far to the north, on the other hand, received little attention. As far as we know, there were no hermits or pilgrims from the general population there either, as in Tibet and the Chinese heartland. It was only with the discussions at court of the eighteenth century that attitudes began to change. Korean intellectuals now increasingly travelled as far as Paektusan and recorded their nature and physical-spiritual experiences in writing. Mountain-related ideas from the big neighbouring country played a more important role in these than in the aforementioned foundation stories.[11]

In contrast, from the nineteenth century onwards this search for origins became highly significant. The background was the political weakness of the Qing dynasty and the rapid rise of Japan to become the dominant military power. In 1905, the Japanese Empire made the Korean peninsula a protectorate, and, five years later, a colony that was to be firmly incorporated. The foreign rulers used aggressive methods to give the population a new identity. In response, Tangun turned into the core symbol of an ethnically conceived Korean nationalism. He became the much-regarded progenitor, which gave the crater mountain a new weight. For example, the intellectual Choe Nam-seon (1890–1957), a leading member of the anti-Japanese independence movement in its early phase, diligently propagated the reputation of Tangun, insisting on his age, which gave Korea a 5,000-year past. While Japanese intellectuals dismissed the narrative as the monk's historical invention, Choe Nam-seon embedded it in Asia's rich shamanistic folk culture and thus contributed in no small way to its popularisation.[12]

After the division of Korea, the tradition split. Since 1949, South Korea has celebrated its National Foundation Day, 'The Day the Sky Opened' (*gaecheonjeol*), when hymns are sung about Tangun as the father of the country. Soon, however, a debate began about his historicity and significance. How should he be portrayed in school textbooks? Is he a religious or just a secular figure? When the president wanted to erect a huge statue of Tangun in Seoul in 1966 for political profiling, evangelical Christians fought back. Although they were also staunch anti-communists, they believed in their literal interpretation of the Bible and classified the worship of a nature deity as idolatry. After further conflicts, from 1999 onwards things escalated. This time the question was whether Tangun statues could be erected in schools in order to turn the youth into real Koreans.[13] The emotionalisation of the founding deity increased interest in the remote volcano in the North, which can only be accessed by South Koreans via China, as North Korea does not issue travel permits to reach it.

In the Stalinist-influenced northern part of the country, after partition Tangun was initially regarded as a primitive relic of the feudal era, incompatible with 'communist progress'. But with the turn towards an ultra-nationalist course, the figure reappeared, this time materially. In 1993, North Korea's *People's Daily* surprisingly announced that archaeologists had unearthed the skeleton of the founding father Tangun near Pyongyang. The (unverifiable) bones were ceremonially buried in a mausoleum and dated to a good 3,000 years BCE.[14]

Sacred Revolution in North Korea

The Kim family has been in power in North Korea since the end of the Second World War. They have already managed to pass on the leadership position to the next generation twice (1994 and 2011). It is a real communist dynasty, but without a fixed rule of succession.[15] The basis was formed by the struggle against Japan and the role that the new supreme father Kim Il-sung (1912–1994) was able to assume and retrospectively establish for himself. In this context, the Paektusan took on another, increasingly prominent role. In the national anthem of North Korea, composed shortly before the country's division in 1948, the 'spirit of Paektusan' is invoked to support the country on its glorious path. When the anthem was replaced more and more by the *Song of General Kim Il-sung* in 1980, the volcano remained topical – but now as the scene of the anti-Japanese guerrilla struggle: the blood flowed red down the mountain, they sang collectively; the flowers bloomed red there and proclaimed the glory of the world-famous general. Later, Paektusan made an appearance in the North Korean emblem, which, according to the constitution, shows 'a grand hydroelectric power station under Mt. Paektu, the sacred mountain of the revolution, and the beaming light of a five-pointed red star with ears of rice forming an oval frame'.[16]

In Kim Il-sung's many-volume autobiography, written by him and/or his aides shortly before his death, the mountain appears in various phases. We may assume that these *Reminiscences* did not primarily serve to establish historical truth, but they did not remain entirely free of reality either. Kim Il-sung spent his school years in Manchuria, where his family had fled. There he joined the anti-Japanese youth movement and later the Chinese Communist Party. Around 1928, he apparently went with comrades from the movement to a remote village at the foot of Paektusan. There, 99 deities were believed to have descended from heaven to bathe in the crater lake and ascend back to heaven. The village built a temple with 99 rooms, which people visited twice a year to offer prayers. A comrade of Kim Il-sung's remarked that Karl Marx was right: religion was opium for the people. Kim Il-sung replied, according to his *Reminiscences*, that one should not take such a narrow view. What was important was the fact that the people in the temple invoked divine punishments for Japan.[17]

Several times in this late work, the mountain is also given a general purpose. For example: 'As Mt. Paektu, an ancestral mountain, commands all the mountains in Korea, so the anti-Japanese armed struggle we started and developed in the forests of Mt. Paektu formed the mainstream of our people's struggle for national liberation and social progress.'[18] The statements hint at the Korean doctrine of descent without naming Tangun, and immediately switch to the struggle against the Japanese colonial rulers. This formed the new founding myth and trump card for Kim Il-sung. As a guerrilla leader in the anti-Japanese army organised by Chinese communists, he played a prominent role in the 1930s. After their defeat, he defected to the Soviet Union and became an officer in the Red Army. It was this army that drove out the Japanese in 1945, and it was not least Joseph Stalin who helped Kim Il-sung to come to power in Pyongyang.[19]

In the 1980s, the country's international situation deteriorated and made it difficult to secure the transfer of power from the 'Great Leader' to his son Kim Jong-il. The idea of the magic mountain and anti-colonialism could be useful for this purpose. The birthplace of Kim Jong-il was moved to the vicinity of Paektusan. In 1987, a log cabin was built there in which the second leader (actually born in the Soviet Union) is said to have seen the light of day. To affirm this, a nearby peak was renamed 'Jong-il Peak'. This also gave the boy a liberator image. A cross-generational connection developed between the ruling family and the newly conjured mountain. Increasingly, people referred to the family as the 'Paektu bloodline'. After power passed to a son again in 2011, the dynastic expression even found its way into the basic law.[20]

The alleged birthplace of the 'Beloved Leader' formed only one element of a vast commemorative infrastructure at Paektusan, which was intended to show the people the importance of the liberation struggle and the leader's family. Although the historical struggle had largely taken place in Manchuria across the Chinese border,[21] the 'secret guerrilla camps' were now supposedly discovered and restored on the Korean side. Armies of students, soldiers and factory workers of both sexes have since made pilgrimages to the heroic mountain landscape and allowed themselves to be seized by the revolutionary Paektusan spirit. A publication from 2015 cites the figure of 63 million visits in the past decades.[22] The fact that images of the Paektusan are present throughout the country certainly contributes to the emotional impact: on public buildings, during important announcements on television, as backgrounds at state occasions and on product packaging.

However, as the Tangun symbolism lives on beneath the Kim symbolism, the mountain is also a unifying element, depending on the situation. When a film crew from the Alpine Museum of Switzerland met a construction worker from Pyongyang on the summit in 2019 and asked him about his motives, he said: 'I came here to look at Paektusan, the sacred mountain of the revolution, the home of the Korean people and the mountain of reconciliation.' In the West, people tend to give little credence to such statements, which sound like official slogans. However, a distinction must also be made here. Recently, a North Korean refugee was asked whether the exuberant expressions of grief at the passing of Kim Jong-il in 2011 were genuine, as these appeared bizarre in Western eyes. The North Korean candidly said that tears had to be feigned at that moment, as the second Kim had lacked popularity after the past crises. A real shock, however, was the death of the first Kim in 1994. At that time, people thought the end of the world had come; they offered each other their condolences and 'everyone prayed desperately for his return'.[23]

Religious Mountain Worship in Asia

Is it a religious act when the population of an atheist state prays for the return of their leader? How religious are scholars and literati when they light incense in a Confucius temple for the sage who has become immortal? And what are we to make of Western tourists who, by their own admission, take part in a Buddhist mountain circumambulation out of spiritual interest? The sacred-religious sphere is difficult to separate from the secular, just as it is difficult to separate economy from society or politics from culture. Precise empirical observations are usually more fruitful than general demarcations: certain words, gestures, symbols, forms of organisation, the specialised religious personnel, the perception and traditional stories of supernatural powers, miracles and deities, together with their reference to place. This allows us to grasp a certain 'family resemblance' in the religious, which is often more interesting for historical research than theoretically prefabricated definitions.[24]

Under such methodological premises, we have made historical visits to a handful of sacred mountains in Asia in the first five chapters of this book (Tsari and Kailash in Tibet, the Chinese mountain systems with their main peak Tai Shan, and most recently Paektusan). Depending on the context, considerable variety has come to light. One could easily extend the selection, for everything points to the fact that sacred mountains were and are widespread in Asia. Their visibility certainly also has to do with the early emergence of writing in these cultures. In addition to the countless candidates mentioned in the literature for such an extension of the selection, there are two qualitative indications of cultural peculiarities of this part of the world: (1) the system of sacred state mountains, established in China and radiating from there, seems to be without a real counterpart anywhere in the world,[25] and (2) the same can be said of the specialised mountain religiosity known as *Shugendo* ('path to magical powers') in Japan, which emerged from the blending of Buddhist currents with Indigenous cults; it also formed an early type of mountaineering.[26]

For all their diversity, the examples of religious mountain worship in Asia studied also show clear parallels: in all cases, their extent increased during the modern era, whether at the beginning of the period, or only since the nineteenth century or later. It was a long-term growth phenomenon. One should not, in principle, outsource such forms of religious practice to early historical phases about which little or nothing is known in detail. Mircea Eliade's archaic figure of *homo religiosus* is not very helpful for research (see Chapter 2). However, the examples also show clear indications of secularisation and a decrease in religious intensity, for example in revolutionary caesuras or in profane tourism.

Paektusan – Sacred Mountain of the Revolution

In general, secularisation has been an important trend in this age of globalisation. Cult communities have been subject to loosening or dissolution due to rapidly increasing contacts. An example from our context is the eclectic connections of Buddhist currents with sophisticated, secular lifestyles. The trend, however, has not led to an all-round renunciation of the 'sacred', but remains interspersed with counter-trends: newly formed communities could, and can, take on a religious character of their own.[27] More on such questions is offered in the conclusion of this book (Chapter 11). For now, we expand our horizons through further travels on other continents.

~ 6 ~

RISE OF THE CHRISTIAN CROSSES

The religious significance of the mountains in Europe can be considered by means of the Christian cross. It is a comparatively unambiguous symbol that recalls the sacrificial death of the Saviour Jesus Christ and thus addresses a central message of his church. Materially made crosses are also locatable and can serve as an indicator of the sacredness of a particular space. However, crosses can be used for a wide variety of purposes. In the world of legends, for example, they often protected against harmful magic and against witches, to whom magic was attributed. This observation is not unimportant because, since the nineteenth century, the opinion has arisen that there used to be a kind of counter-sanctity in witchcraft, especially in the mountains.[1] This opinion arose from the romanticisation and reinterpretation of historic folk culture. It gained in certainty with the modern witchcraft movement, in which women in particular turned the traditional, negative image of witches into a positive one and used it to channel a feminist spirituality in organised groups and workshops. One of the first of these self-confident 'covens' is said to have met in Los Angeles in 1972. In contrast, historical research has found no evidence that the (imagined) witches' sabbath exuded any particular sanctity since its invention in the fifteenth century. So, it is not the case that a high concentration of witches in the mountains (not documented either) could have contributed greatly to their religious significance.[2]

As explained in the introductory chapters, Christianity paid little attention to the mountains from the time of its institutionalisation in late antiquity. In contrast, clergy and scholars spent a lot of energy on the question of how to interpret the prohibition of images in the Mosaic commandments. 'Thou shalt not make unto thee any graven image', it says in the Decalogue of various Bible versions. Is the cross, which reminds us of the Christian Redeemer, also such a forbidden image? What should one make of the numerous Christian frescoes, oil paintings, statues, crosses and crucifixes (crosses with the body of the crucified)? These questions arose again in the sixteenth century, first in Reformation circles.

Iconoclastic Controversies

Andreas Karlstadt, professor in Wittenberg and a fellow campaigner of Martin Luther, arrived at a critical conclusion and called for the destruction of religious images in 1522. His extensive pamphlet *On the Dismissal of the Images* (*Von Abtuhung der Bylder*), which was widely read in the German-speaking world, portrayed them as idolatry. According to Karlstadt, images of saints, for example, did not show the divine essence, but merely the physical appearance of the saints, which suppressed access to God in the heart. The veneration of such 'carnal' images and statues turned the churches into 'whorehouses'. The veneration of images of Christ as a dying man should also be rejected. 'From the image of Christ crucified you learn nothing but the earthly suffering of Christ in the flesh, how Christ bows his head and the like.' In the Bible, however, the Saviour said that his flesh was of no use, that it was the spirit that counted and conferred life. Even in special situations, these images remained mute and deaf, which is why Karlstadt advised against 'the dying clinging to carved or painted crucifixes'.[3]

Luther did not share Karlstadt's opinion. He rejected the idea that one could attain salvation by endowing pious images. But their use as didactic tools should be permitted. In the Zurich and Geneva Reformation and in many other places in northern Europe, however, the more radical interpretations found favour. In various forms, iconoclasm swept through cities and countries that turned away from the old church. On the orders of Reformed theologians and authorities or through the initiative of activists, representations of the Son of God and the saints were removed from churches in the sixteenth and seventeenth centuries and in some cases destroyed. Their veneration was now considered idolatry in the areas concerned. This banishment also affected crucifixes and crosses outside church buildings – in public squares, streets, at forks in the road and in fields. The sacred became more abstract in the Reformed world, less tangible spatially.[4] If there should ever be a movement to erect summit crosses, it would certainly not originate here.

The Catholic answer to the controversial question of images was formulated by the Council of Trent (see Chapter 1). At its meeting on 3 December 1563, it stated that the images of Jesus, the Blessed Virgin Mary and other saints should continue to be venerated, but not because one should believe 'that there is a divinity or a power in them because of which they are to be venerated, or as if something were to be asked of them or confidence placed in the images, as the pagans used to do'. Whoever kisses the images of Christ and bows before them with his head uncovered should worship the Lord, not his image. For the

Iconoclastic Controversies

members of the Church, they were also instructions in the faith and salutary models for the conduct of life. However, one must avoid 'anything salacious' and not allow figures 'with seductive beauty'.[5]

After the Council, regulation and renewal of the sacred space in the church and settlement began, at an earlier or later date, depending on the region. The bishops had to visit, control and admonish their congregations regularly. When the new Bishop of Grenoble made his first pastoral visit in the Western Alps in 1672, the church bells announced his arrival in each place. The local priest received the bishop and his entourage at the parish boundary and presented him with the parish cross, to which the high visitor paid his respects with a kiss and a bow. Afterwards, they solemnly went to the village – first the horsemen, behind them the priest with the cross, then the clergy and nobles with the bishop under a canopy. In the church book of one village, the bishop discovered notes on blessings for field crosses. The sayings were unauthorised and could seem like magical formulas, so he stopped them. In general, however, crosses and crucifixes played an increasingly important role in the landscape. Even Alpine settlements at high altitudes, which were only inhabited in summer, were increasingly furnished with them. This was the birth of a Catholic-Baroque sacred landscape, which, however, only reached the cultivated areas and not the summit region of the mountains.[6]

In Grenoble and other dioceses of the Roman Church, chapels in remote places and at high altitudes were often dedicated to Saint Michael. According to the Bible (Book of Joshua), the canonised archangel had vanquished Satan in dragon form and cast him into hell. In the Orthodox Church of Eastern Europe, on the other hand, Elijah, the prophet from the Book of Kings, was the saint associated with mountains. According to the Scriptures, a storm wind carried Elijah to heaven in a fiery chariot.[7] In Greece – long under the rule of the Sunni Islamic Ottomans – there are quite a number of mountains named Profitis Ilias. This is particularly striking in comparison to Western and Central Europe, where mountains rarely bear the names of saints. In the Alps, for example, only a handful of such names are counted among some 1,300 main peaks, and these were mostly transferred to the summit from settlements below.[8] In Greece, the Ilias mountains seem to have been associated above all with the monastic movement and the numerous mountain monasteries. They had emerged victorious from the early medieval iconoclastic controversy of the Eastern Church and represented a mystically coloured, unscholastic religiosity in which the sign of the cross also played a major role.[9]

The most important centre of this monastic culture was the Holy Mountain of Athos, which still consists of twenty monasteries and many hermitages. The term 'holy' is documented early on and has become common in most languages. The supernatural characteristics of this peninsula, which rises from the Aegean Sea to 2,033 metres, were not central to the settlement of God-seekers in the Middle Ages, however. Rather, its seclusion from the world was attractive.[10] The peninsula only acquired a sacred aura through the persistent religious lifestyle of the inhabitants, similar to other Christian mountain monasteries (see Chapter 1). Significantly, the monks and hermits showed little interest in the mountaintop. Athos was only given a summit chapel in 1895 and an associated cross in 1897. Modern currents probably played a part in this: Western alpinism and the summit cross movement had already developed considerable momentum by that time.[11]

The Summits Are Being Christianised

The summit cross movement was initiated by enlightened Catholic clergy and religiously minded Enlightenment thinkers. It started from the early modern developments of the Roman Church just described. But at the beginning of the Romantic period, Christianisation went beyond the cultivated landscape to the mountain peaks. The dedication of a summit cross on the Erzberg in Austria in 1823 (Figure 7) was described with these emotional words:

> Awe-inspiring silence reigned among the numerous crowd. Not an eye remained dry with inner emotion. The serene morning sky vaulted, a dome of Sapphir, the vast temple into which the Alpine region was transformed at that moment. A temple built by the hand of the Almighty, the Alps its pillars, the sky its roof!

For the reporter, nature seems to have become a consecrated building, the centre of Christian life. Previously, the priest had preached to a relevant psalm ('Mountains and all hills, praise the Lord!') and held high Mass. Afterwards trumpets and timpani set in; the echo of the music and the salutes of honour were returned from other mountains. 'And bowing down before the unveiled cross lay the glory of the earth, and all hearts lifted up joyfully and in the spirit of love to Him who is, was, and shall be.'[12]

The Summits Are Being Christianised

Figure 7. Inauguration of the Holy Cross on the Erzberg in 1823 (pen and ink drawing).

Since this early period, summit crosses have proliferated continuously, right up to the present day. Even before that, of course, there were crosses in some prominent locations.[13] However, the two summit crosses on the Kleinglockner and Großglockner from 1799 and 1800 are regarded as prototypes that were also publicised and thus able to trigger imitation effects. Crosses became much more frequent in the twentieth century with the popularisation of mountaineering, and they reached a temporary peak in the last decades. In the Alpine region, to which we will limit ourselves for the time being, the number of summit crosses is currently estimated at several thousand.[14] In the beginning, they were a religious-cultural concomitant of mountain exploration and the alpinism that emerged from it (see Chapter 2). In order to set a dynamic tradition in motion, however, a confessional milieu was needed. In outline, three regions and phases can be identified: (1) Habsburg Austria in the nineteenth century, with strong feudal components; (2) Italy since the transition into the twentieth century, with strong religious and ecclesiastical components; (3) individual regions such as the 'holy land of Tyrol' and the Catholic 'citadel' of Fribourg in mixed-denomination Switzerland, with the practice initially religiously charged, then taken over by secular associations and circles of friends.[15]

Rise of the Christian Crosses

Of particular interest for the question of the religious significance of mountains is the aforementioned Italian contribution, triggered by the nationwide project for the Jubilee Year 1900 with a network of large summit crosses in honour of *Cristo Redentore* (Christ the Redeemer). The project will be discussed separately in the following chapter. At this point I will pick out a few revealing episodes from the multi-faceted history of the summit crosses, especially in Austria.

The initiative for the two Glockner crosses in 1799 and 1800 came from an enlightened prince-bishop with an interest in alpinism. These were large-scale first ascents and scientific expeditions, which also claimed the highest mountain in the area, and its secondary peak, for the church. A few years earlier, the Revolution in France had desecrated and cleared out the churches (see Chapter 1), and shortly afterwards Napoleon's armies were in the middle of Austria. Holding up the cross in this situation was also a political act.[16] The plan for the aforementioned summit cross of 1823 on the Erzberg, on the other hand, came from a secular source, namely from Archduke Johann, a younger brother of the Emperor. With his many initiatives and ideals, he was at the beginning of a process that can be called the monarchisation of the Alps. The summit cross was a statement against modern unbelief and at the same time intended to benefit progress in mining, by allegedly protecting the Erzberg, which means 'Mountain of Minerals'.[17] How important the monarchy became for the summit crosses was subsequently shown by the cross dedications on imperial anniversaries. Dynastic crises could also play a role, as in Bavaria, where a summit cross commemorated the former king Ludwig I in 1886, shortly after the current king Ludwig II had been deprived of power and died.[18]

A wave of religious mountain markers followed after the Second World War. The Dutch chaplain Karl Loven, an enthusiastic alpinist and photographer, who officiated in a mountain community south of Innsbruck, became well known and gave the impetus for the erection of several summit crosses. As a rule, he was able to win over the village and valley youth, including returned soldiers of the Wehrmacht. This was the case in 1947 on the 3,507-metre-high Zuckerhütl in the Stubai Alps: as usual, the youth carried the iron cross, which had been made in individual parts, in several stages to the summit, where it was assembled and erected. At the inauguration Mass, the chaplain emphasised that the sign stood in thanksgiving for the sparing of the valley from the ravages of war, in atonement for the summit crosses destroyed by the National Socialists in previous years and as a plea for peace. The following year, Loven also prompted the melodramatic mountain film *Summit Cross* (*Gipfelkreuz*), and in 1951 he published the novel *The Summit Cross: Youth in Struggle and Probation* (*Das Gipfelkreuz. Jugend in Kampf und Bewährung*).[19]

Not far from the Stubai Alps are the Volderstal and the Navistal, separated by the 2,619-metre-high Sonnenspitze. The two valleys can only be reached by car in a roundabout way, so they have little to do with each other in the motorised age. Without consultation, associations on either side of the Sonnenspitze came up with the same idea for the same year (1995). In Volders it was the mountain running team and in Navis the *Trachtenverein* (traditional costume association). Since the mountain runners were a few weeks faster, the astonished and irritated Trachtenverein had to place its cross on a secondary peak. By now, for an active association, placing crosses was part of good manners in Tyrol, only attracting attention in this case because the matter had not been discussed and well-oiled in the inn beforehand (which a letter to the editor subsequently called for).[20] The church had stopped providing the impetus. Under these conditions, the symbols could also cross denominational boundaries. The Protestant Lower Engadine, which adjoins Tyrol to the west, received its first and still only summit cross shortly before 2000. It was offered to the community by a sawmill company and flown up the mountain by helicopter.[21]

In the Crossfire of Criticism

Summit crosses have provoked opposition from early on and especially in recent times. The controversies say something about the meaning that these Christian monuments might hold for the population. Perhaps it is significant that in the cultural sphere such a case occurred even before summit crosses became a tradition. At the end of 1808, the painter Caspar David Friedrich exhibited a painting entitled *Cross in the Mountains* in his Dresden flat (Figure 8). The ornate frame was adorned with several angel heads and the triangular Eye of God. It is unclear whether the painting was intended for a chapel. In any case, the art critic Basilius von Ramdohr reacted with vehement reproaches. His detailed review adhered to landscape painting of the seventeenth and eighteenth centuries and common sacred art. According to him, the painting violated central norms. It was presumptuous 'when landscape painting wants to creep into churches and crawl onto altars'. The traditional 'true religion of Christ' differed from the newly emerged mysticism 'with its languishing worship of the cross'. The spat, which has gone down in art history as the Ramdohr controversy, continued for several rounds and gives an idea of how sensitive certain relationships between religion and nature were at the beginning of the Romantic period.[22]

Figure 8. 'Cross in the Mountains' by Caspar David Friedrich, 1808.

According to current knowledge, a line of conflict that continues to this day opened up after the First World War. In some regions, summit crosses had become established, and many young alpinists, who wanted to surpass the older ones in daring and were committed to new ideals of nature, moved to the mountains. Among their role models was Eugen Guido Lammer, who had made a name for himself by solo mountaineering and was also active as a journalist at an early stage. In 1928, Lammer described everything that had been placed on the summits 'in blind development mania' as disturbing: plaques, flags, boundary stones, cairns and, last but not least, crosses – every 'work of man' ought to be removed in favour of an unadulterated experience of nature.[23] In the National Socialist milieu, his view soon took on an additional anti-church thrust and led to repeated cross destructions from around 1935 onwards. In the postwar period, the idealistic reference to nature was able to hold on and gain strength again so that, towards the end of the twentieth century, an increasing ecological awareness was confronted with an increasing number of crosses. Lammer's question became more topical: 'What does the cross have to say in the mountain wilderness?' [24]

The latent tension led to a series of violent incidents involving the clandestine removal or destruction of summit symbols. Quite a sensation was caused by the mountain guide Patrick Bussard, who confessed in 2010 to having brought down three summit crosses in the canton of Fribourg. He stated on record that nature had no religion and that he wanted to shake the power of the church by doing so. Until the 1950s, Catholicism had a firm grip on the faithful in this canton and competed imperiously against the zeitgeist in 'popular missions'. Bussard was tried primarily for violating freedom of religion and worship. Officially, he had the freethinkers on his side, who disputed the violation and raised the question of the building permit. During the trial, two plaintiffs withdrew, but Bussard was fined. In a newspaper interview, the diocese's vicar general said the cross represented not only a religion, but also humanity. He also stated that the cultural heritage was permeated by countless Christian symbols that made up the identity of the region. For example, the edelweiss on the traditional costume stands for the idea of eternity, that is, for God. This bold interpretation suggests that the vicar had no theological justification for summit crosses, but knew that the weight of regional history was on his side.[25]

Shortly afterwards, an illustrated book about Fribourg's summit crosses was published, which strongly relativised the religious side. In the title, the author even avoided the word cross and replaced it with 'presence'. According to the preface, this spiritual presence was pluralistic, but remained an active force: 'For these crosses speak. They are alive. And each of them tells its story.'[26] In the real world, however, they may have lacked an audience. According to Hans-Joachim Löwer, who recently visited a hundred or more summit crosses in the Alps in person, mountaineers are usually not interested in them: 'The aesthetics, the message, the story they tell – all this falls flat.'[27] In this way, the summit crosses share the fate of many monuments in the cities of Europe, which also receive only sporadic attention. Once erected, public interest fades until, at best, there is a change or controversy. Unlike the churches of human settlements, continuous forms of cult, such as periodic pilgrimages, developed around the remote summit crosses only exceptionally. This considerably limited their religious significance.

Rise of the Christian Crosses

A few years before Bussard's provocation, four alpinists from Milan chose a different path. They installed a 130-centimetre Buddha statue on a difficult-to-climb mountain on the border between Italy and Switzerland. Prayer flags had earlier heralded the arrival of the Indian founder of his religion in several areas. With globalisation, Tibetan Buddhism in particular offered itself as a worldwide mountain religion (see Chapter 3). The alpinists assured the media that the undertaking was a bit of fun, but also a serious protest against the 'pollution' caused by the many summit crosses. 'There is a holy war on the summits', a major evening newspaper commented on 9 September 2005 on the fierce debate that broke out between Christian and other opponents. The Alpine Buddha, however, soon turned out to be a 'Hotei', who in the West is often confused with the enlightened one and is known as the laughing or fat Buddha. So, the Milanese climbers do not seem to have had any deeper religious knowledge or intentions.[28] The fact that they could accuse the summit crosses of an 'inappropriate flourish' (*smisurata fioritura*) was due in no small part to a major Italian Jubilee project, which is discussed in the next chapter.

~ 7 ~

THE REDEEMER IN THE ITALIAN MOUNTAINS

The most extensive ecclesiastical-religious investment in summit crosses was connected with the Jubilee Year 1900, which, starting from the Holy See in Rome, was to be celebrated by Catholics all over the world and caused a massive mobilisation, especially in Italy. 'Jubilee Years' or 'Holy Years' had a centuries-long tradition in the Roman Church. By means of special regulations, indulgences and pilgrimages, they offered a recurring opportunity to bind the faithful more closely to the Pope and his court. The fact that a special mountain project was also initiated for 1900 was due, among other things, to the emergence of a 'Catholic Alpinism'. The Italian historian Marco Cuaz has impressively described this current in a series of publications.[1]

In the early days of their passion, alpinists from the cities and other countries often found shelter with clergymen in the mountain villages who could not only entertain them but also accompany them. Many of them were interested in mountain research as long as it remained within the familiar framework of 'Christian science' and did not clash with the writings of the Church. Soon after the proclamation of the new Kingdom of Italy in 1861, an Alpine Club was formed in Turin, which later became the Club Alpino Italiano. It gave strong impetus to mountaineering in the surrounding regions, but due to its elitist, secular orientation it was also an impetus for Catholics to seek their own paths. As early as the mid-nineteenth century, the physical training and disciplining of youth in the outdoors had been recommended and organised by Catholic educators. Later, youth excursions took on forms of moderate alpinism, which, under the guidance of priests, could also include families, women and older parishioners and lead to nearby, tame mountains. The occasions combined the enjoyment of nature and sociability with religious services. They were a religious response to the 'materialistic' high mountain alpinism that had emerged.

In addition, some *preti alpinisti* (alpinist priests) themselves strove to reach the heights and occasionally erected their first crosses up there. Soon the idea of celebrating Holy Mass in the high Alps spread. On 11 August 1893, three priests from the Aosta Valley celebrated Mass on Mont Blanc, 4,808 metres above sea level, with permission from the authorities and a consecrated altar stone carried up there. According to one of the clergymen, this highest peak in the Alps now ceased to be a profane mountain. It had been transformed and became 'the Lord's footstool; the mountain where he wanted to settle for a moment; a mountain where it pleases God to make his dwelling (*Mons in quo beneplacitum est Deo habitare in eo*).'[2]

An Idea for the Jubilee Year 1900

Conflicts between the emerging European nation states and the Roman Church were frequent in the second half of the nineteenth century. In Italy, they took on more acute forms because the new, unified kingdom moved its capital to Rome in 1871 and before that had incorporated the Papal State (it was not recognised as sovereign again, in a diminished form, until 1929). Against this background, clerics and staunch Catholics perceived many measures of the new state as anti-clerical and anti-religious. The mysterious Freemasons, described as the arch-enemies of the Church, were also seen at work everywhere. In this tense situation, religious action associations such as the *Gioventù cattolica italiana* (Catholic Youth of Italy) and the *Opera dei congressi cattolici* (Works of Catholic Conferences) were formed. A driving force of this movement was Giovanni Acquaderni (1839–1922) from Bologna. He distinguished himself especially in the organisation of celebrations on a grand scale in honour of the Pope. Without him, the Jubilee Year 1900 would probably have been celebrated differently.[3]

Acquaderni came from a noble family and developed into a successful religious entrepreneur who always found new ways to intensify spiritual and material communication among his clientele. The basis – as with similar entrepreneurs in other countries – was modern journalism. With high-circulation denominational magazines, pictures and devotional objects, he created an efficient means of advancing into the highest ecclesiastical circles. The affinity with modernism was particularly evident in his great Jubilee exhibitions, which brought religious art objects from all countries and thus a touch of the World's Fairs to the Vatican. The enterprising Acquaderni was regularly able to lay large sums of money from the faithful at the feet of the Holy See as *Denaro di S. Pietro* (Peter's Pence) or *Obolo dell'amor figliale* (Donation of filial love). The popes thanked him with orders and titles, from the *Ordine Piano* (Pian Order) to the title of *Conte* (Count). At his death, he was again showered with honours. On his deathbed, he consoled himself with a crucifix that a grandson had recently brought him from Rome, personally blessed by the Holy Father.[4]

As a seasoned large-scale organiser, Acquaderni set his sights on the year 1900 early on. He saw it as an opportunity to celebrate 1900 years of Jesus Christ and, at the same time, to highlight his living *Augusto Vicario* (Exalted Vicar) in the person of Pope Leo XIII. But he had not reckoned with the Congregation of Rites, which had long exercised control over jubilees. In a letter dated 14 May 1895, the prefect of this Vatican authority pointed out that centenary celebrations were a new invention that should not be applied to the 'mysteries of our Holy Religion'. Later he was more explicit: the Jubilees had always been times of penance and must remain so, which the *centenaristi* (centenary adherents), in their excessive zeal, did not see. Acquaderni bowed as always 'in absolute obedience'. But he had highly placed comrades-in-arms in the Vatican, and soon the prefect was promoted to another office. This cleared the way for a major Jubilee event that surpassed all previous ones.[5]

The strategic goal of the preparatory committee, which was also well supported by the church, was to make the twentieth century one that would belong entirely and solely to Jesus Christ. An initial programme outline envisaged a course lasting several years: collection of the donations of *Obolo dell'amor figliale* for Leo XIII; pilgrimages in spirit and/or in reality to Lourdes, Palestine, Loreto, Rome; spiritual retreats and holy missions; lighting up the night of the transition from 1899 to 1900 in the cities with electricity and in the countryside with bonfires. The committee invited bishops and other personalities to bring in their own proposals as well. This was the moment when the mountains came into play. A letter from the local preparatory committee in Rome suggested erecting nineteen crosses for the nineteen centuries on the most important mountains in Italy (see map, Figure 9). Later they added a twentieth cross on the Pope's home mountain and opened up the possibility of erecting statues instead of just crosses.[6]

Despite numerous competitors, the proposal managed to be included in the programme of the Jubilee Year, to which result the aforementioned Catholic alpinism may well have contributed. A circular letter of 1899 underlined the appropriateness of the idea: 'The high mountain peaks which tower over the Italian regions form very suitable places for the erection of an imperishable memorial of solemn homage to the Saviour.' A map of Italy showed the mountains chosen, from Monviso and Mombarone in Piedmont to Monte San Giuliano in Sicily.[7] On 23 December 1900, the Pope received the most prominent committee members, who presented him with twenty inscribed stone blocks from the selected mountains. To commemorate the event, these were to be walled in at the Holy Door of St Peter's Basilica, which is only open during the Jubilee years. What happened to them subsequently does not seem to be on record. I have been told by a Roman colleague that the search for the stones has so far been fruitless; when the wall was knocked out in following Jubilee years, they could have been thrown away, sold or given away.[8]

Figure 9. *Map of the summit crosses planned in honour of Christ the Redeemer in Italy, 1899.*

Cristo Redentore and the Holy Book of Nature

The solemn handing over of these mementos preceded the erection of the crosses. In fact, on the occasion of the ceremony, only two of the twenty monuments planned to pay homage to the Saviour and his Vicar yet stood on the Italian mountains. Subsequently, others were added; the last one came ten years after the date. Four announced summit crosses fell by the wayside altogether and were never realised.[9]

In fact, much depended on the zeal of the local dioceses and parishes. The central committee only provided the framework; the execution and financing took place at the lower levels. The monument on the Mombarone in Piedmont developed into a showcase project. The clergy was committed to it, as were a considerable number of the faithful. The collection of money resulted in a proud 42,000 lire, thanks in great part to contributions from women and aristocrats. With this, a representative bronze statue of Jesus with the cross could be realised. Apparently, the Pope himself had advised this when the bishop was in Rome. Such a statue could withstand the centuries and also bear witness to the faith of the ancestors to the children's children. (Two generations later, it was badly damaged by lightning and vandalism). It is beyond my knowledge why and at what stage the projects failed in four cases. Instead, triggered by the Jubilee Year, numerous other summit crosses were added that the committee had not planned for. Obviously, quite a few people felt involved and encouraged. The feelings and possibilities on the ground were decisive.[10]

Occasionally, the warning against overly daring undertakings – a central maxim of Catholic alpinism – was also thrown to the wind. A spectacular erection took place on 24 September 1902 on the Matterhorn, whose ascent had already cost many lives. However, the spiritual leader of the four-man team belonged to the elite of the *preti alpinisti* and not only managed to hoist the iron cross to the top with his men and fix it there but also celebrated Holy Mass on the narrow summit ridge of the Italian side for his small congregation, free from giddiness. A cross on a mountain makes you feel more Christian and faithful, he wrote in his report. Prayer comes directly from the heart. There is something imposing about a Mass at this sublime height, where the priest commands whole nations, and is closer to the divine. 'I don't know if one can dream of anything more wonderful.'[11]

Pope Leo XIII was probably not familiar with these feelings, if only because he was very old. At the age of 90, he wrote an encyclical dedicated to the Redeemer for the Jubilee Year (*Tametsi futura prospicientibus*). Even if one could not look into the future without worry, he said, by God's grace there had been a spark of hope in recent years: signs of the revival of faith in a time of class struggle and the secular state, which could be met through the divine mediation of the Cristo Redentore. The Pope addressed many things that moved him at this threshold of time, from the original sin of the human race to the indispensable role of the Church. Those who strive for a Christianity to their own taste with lenient rules must, he wrote, keep the Cross before their eyes, 'the model of our life, the eternal standard of all who wish to follow Christ in reality and not merely in name'.[12]

Leo XIII's cross had no concrete place in the world. His encyclical dealt exclusively with the history of salvation. The Pope did not open the 'book of nature', which revealed God's activity in the beauty and usefulness of the environment. This is a further indication that the culture of piety in the mountains was fed by other sources. It was mainly the lower clergy in the periphery and the nature-loving parishioners, that is, the basis of Catholic alpinism, who developed and practised it in the late nineteenth and early twentieth centuries. They usually did not go so far as to claim that their mountains were sacred.[13] But, in the eyes of many, holiness was also a quality transmitted through touch. Acquaderni, the grey eminence of the Jubilee Year, had used this principle time and again. In order to spur his fellow Catholics to increase their contributions in favour of the Pope, he used to raffle off among active church institutions the church equipment that the Holy Father had used the previous year.[14] Thus, for believers, the holy crosses and statues on the mountains may also have possessed a charisma at times.

The Jubilee of 1900 was not an internal Italian event, it was addressed to the faithful of the 'universal Church'. In the period of European high imperialism and accelerated globalisation, the Church felt even more universal than before. Indeed, numerous summit crosses and summit statues were built around the globe. The most famous follow-up project was the *Cristo Redentor* on Corcovado above Rio de Janeiro. It was proposed in 1921 by the Catholic circle of the Brazilian capital. The small local Baptist congregation called the idea idolatry, in keeping with their Reformation forebears who had admonished 400 years before that one should not create and worship images of God. For the vast majority of Christians, the objection was also obsolete, because the modern technical design of the religious monument inspired the national pride of the young Republic. The thirty-metre-high Art Deco figure was made in Paris between 1922 and 1931. When financing became a problem, the Vatican lent a hand. At the inauguration ceremony, the famous inventor Guglielmo Marconi

Cristo Redentore and the Holy Book of Nature

switched on the electrical lighting of the monument in Rio de Janeiro via radio waves from Italy, also to remind us 'where the centre of Christendom lies'.[15]

~ 8 ~

SIX GRANDFATHERS AND OTHER AMERICAN MOUNTAINS

The Black Hills are a mountain range that rises like an island 1,200 metres above the prairie landscape of South Dakota in the Midwest of the USA. The area is distinguished from the dry, often yellowish grassland of the plains by its dark forest cover. The uppermost point, long known as Harney Peak, is 2,208 metres above sea level and considered the highest peak east of the Rocky Mountains. In the surrounding area of the Black Hills there are other striking rock formations, such as the almost vertical monolith Devils Tower known in Lakota as *Mato Tipi-la* (Bear Lodge).

On 30 May 1931, Black Elk, a medicine man of the Lakota Sioux who inhabited this area, climbed Harney Peak with companions. He was 68 years old and as a boy had experienced the bloody wars with the advancing US cavalry. At the top, he put on some traditional clothes and began to pray to the 'Six Grandfathers'. He held up his right hand in prayer, and with his left he offered them his pipe, decorated with ribbons and an eagle feather. He referred to the Six Grandfathers as the spiritual powers of the four cardinal points and the two directions up to the firmament and down to the earth. Together they symbolised the entire universe. 'My Grandfathers, the six, may you behold me', began one section of his long invocation. 'You have made me intercessor of my people and you have given a way of living to my people. Where the sun goes down you have presented to me a pipe, that through this pipe I should make my offerings.'[1]

Black Elk (1863–1950) served for many years as a catechist for the Catholic Mission and was also known in this capacity as a reliable, religious man. The prayer on Harney Peak formed a reenactment of a spiritual vision he had experienced as a boy in a fever dream, and which accompanied him throughout his life. It took place as the final act of a long conversation in which he opened up his Native American beliefs and experiences to an American poet and anthropologist.[2] Black Elk's accounts reflect only one of several religious or religion-like views that can be grasped around the ridge. This diversity makes the example particularly interesting as an illustration of the American context. And because the USA rose to become the leading world power of the twentieth century, the images and ideas from this area had a great, international impact.

Superhuman Presidents on Mount Rushmore

Six Grandfathers (*Tunkasila Sakpe Paha*) is also the name of a mountain in the Black Hills. In 1980, the US Board on Geographic Names, which is responsible for the country's toponymy, listed it as the Lakota name for a peak that officially bears the name Mount Rushmore. Fifty years earlier, only the latter name had been recorded and approved by the Board. It referred to an East Coast businessman who had come to the Black Hills in the wake of the gold rush and often went there to hunt. In 1925, he had donated a considerable sum for a monumental sculpture that was to give the mountain a new face and was then in the planning phase.[3]

Between 1927 and 1941, a large workforce used dynamite to blast the faces of four American presidents out of the granite rock, each about eighteen metres high. George Washington, Thomas Jefferson, Abraham Lincoln and Theodore Roosevelt have been looking out over the mountain landscape with their heads held high ever since. The large-scale project in South Dakota was supported by private donations and American federal funds. The artistic director was Gutzon Borglum, son of Danish immigrants. The monument soon developed into a world-renowned tourist site and national enterprise, attracting first thousands and later millions of visitors. At the beginning, however, part of the white settler population was against the project. Some expressed their reservations in quasi-religious language. 'Why should we add to, or rather desecrate, the work of nature with the puny work of man?', one woman wrote to an initiator. 'We love our Black Hills with a love that grows with acquaintance. Leave them to us as nature made them, deep, silent, majestic, natural.' The editor of a local newspaper echoed the same sentiment. 'God's statuary' is superior to any human inspiration.[4]

The proponents also fenced with biblical borrowings. The leading theme of this side, however, became the civil-religious state doctrine of the United States. The presidents symbolised the belief, common among many Americans of European descent, that this was 'God's own country' and that the conquest and seizure of the continent by white immigrants was its 'manifest destiny'. Although only tall men were visible, Rushmore became a 'shrine of democracy' for them.[5] The sculptor Gutzon Borglum (1867–1941) was a vocal proponent of such ideas. Before starting at Mount Rushmore, he had worked in the

South and had been a senior member of the racist Ku Klux Klan. He loved large sculptures and, as a mountaineer, had an affinity for rocky landscapes. He wanted to create a work 'as close to heaven as we can' for posterity. No one had yet adequately depicted 'this irresistible God-man movement' to the American West.[6]

In the summer of 1927, President Calvin Coolidge spent a holiday in the Black Hills and took the opportunity to honour the celebration of the start of construction. 'It will be entirely American in its conception, in its magnitude, in its meaning, and altogether worthy of our country', he said of the emerging Rushmore Monument. It was, he avowed, a true representation of the patriotic spirit. As with most celebrations before 1970, Lakota Indians in feathered regalia also attended the ceremony. Although the intention was to assimilate them as Euro-Americans, 'traditional elements' were in demand on such occasions. There also seems to have been a need on the part of Indians to show themselves in public. Henry Standing Bear (c. 1874–1953), who represented the Lakotas at the ceremony, had earlier received the president on the reservation assigned to his group. In a diplomatically worded speech, he recalled the Indian war leaders of the late nineteenth century who had met violent deaths or been forced to surrender to American arms.[7]

Immortalising this memory was a concern for him later on. In the early 1930s, the idea arose to model the figure of an Indian leader in the Black Hills as a 'response' to the presidents. The choice fell on Crazy Horse, who had helped defeat the seventh US cavalry regiment at Little Big Horn in 1876. But Borglum, boss on Mount Rushmore, would not entertain the request. Henry Standing Bear therefore moved to another mountain peak and received the appropriate permission from the US Forest Service. In 1939, he found a sculptor employed by Borglum who was willing to take the risk. Unlike the large-scale Rushmore construction site, the Crazy Horse Memorial (Figure 10) became a self-supporting family enterprise. But the plans were ambitious: the leader's face was to exceed that of the presidents in height by almost ten metres; he was also to sit on a horse almost 200 metres long. Construction began in 1948; 50 years later, the family had finally blasted the face out of the mountain. It is expected to take generations to complete.[8]

Religious Freedom for Native Americans?

Figure 10. Monument to the Indian leader Crazy Horse in the Black Hills, as of 2020.

There are no more massive mountain carving monuments in the world than those in the Black Hills. Together they are a rock document to a colonialist confrontation. The personified mountains were (and are) admired by the public, but also criticised from many sides. Lakota members, for example, criticised the choice of Crazy Horse, a leader who had refused to be depicted by whites all his life. A few years ago, the *New York Times* described the two heroic monuments as having a strange, out-of-time grandeur.[9] This is one of the many indications that cultic veneration, with its profane and semi-religious components, was losing its intensity. The Indian monument now also appears too much as a knock-off of the 'white America' on Mount Rushmore. This has to do with a tectonic shift in the political-cultural balance of power around 1970. Since then, the question of Indian spirituality has been in the foreground.

Religious Freedom for Native Americans?

There are petroglyphs in the Black Hills that, according to archaeological research, are several thousand years old.[10] However, since the Native Americans got by without writing, the information on early history is sparse. It is known that the Lakotas, a subgroup of the Sioux, settled on the Missouri River in the seventeenth century and later moved westward to the Black Hills area. One reason for this was European immigration to the East Coast, which triggered a chain reaction of east to west movements. At the same time, the horses introduced to the 'New World' spread from the Spanish colonial territory in the south. This allowed the development of a new form of economy. From the late eighteenth century onwards, mounted bison hunting developed into a livelihood for the Lakotas. When rifles reached the small warlike groups via European traders and white settlement, and the US army continued to advance westwards, a zone with a high potential for violence was created.[11]

One of the most famous of all broken treaties between the United States and the Native American nations is the Fort Laramie Treaty of 1868, which granted the Sioux a large reservation area in what is now South Dakota. Shortly afterwards it became known that gold could be found in the Black Hills, and Euro-Americans, accompanied by soldiers, invaded the protected area. Soon after, parts of the reservation, including the Black Hills, were officially annexed – an act that later became a protracted court case (see below). In addition to establishing and dissolving reservations, the government pursued a determined assimilation policy, among other things by supporting Christian mission churches and banning Native rituals. The *Code of Indian Offenses* of 1883 prohibited or restricted religious and cultural ceremonies, especially the Sun Dance, which was important to the community, and the healing practices of the religious specialists, the medicine men. The rituals were considered un-Christian, if not devilish cults. It was often denied that Native Americans had a religion at all.[12]

This may have been a motive for Native leaders not being reluctant to show their rituals in public. When a presidential head was to be dedicated again on Mount Rushmore in 1936 and a visit by the current US president was announced, Black Elk and other Lakotas asked to be able to hold their own event on the summit. They had themselves hoisted up by the factory railway and at the top Black Elk, the aforementioned Catholic medicine man, prayed to the 'Six Grandfathers' in full ceremonial dress. He included the whites in his prayer and also pleaded for rain, green grass and plentiful supplies.[13] Based on his reports and many other sources from the nineteenth and twentieth centuries, the traditional religiosity of this group can be reconstructed in outline. The mountains played a prominent role in it. The young Lakotas, for example, often sought their visions and dream images, which marked their passage to the status of adult men, in remote summit regions. However, the mountains seem to have been only the places and not the addressees of the prayers (this in contrast to some other Indigenous religions on the American double continent).

Controversial Spirituality in National Parks

Whether the entire region of the Black Hills could be called sacred is uncertain. However, there were surely specific places in it that had a sacred character.[14]

In the 1960s, a fundamental critique of society and civilisation began in the USA; the Red Power movement emerged on Native American territory. This changed the cultural power imbalance between the religions. While Christianity was put on the defensive and under pressure to conform, Native spirituality was now propagated vigorously. In 1970 and 1971, activists of the American Indian Movement occupied the Rushmore memorial. Unlike before, they did not ask anyone for permission. On the mountaintop, they didn't only perform Indigenous rituals. One leader shouted down the Christian Ten Commandments to the audience in a loud resounding voice and added as an eleventh commandment: 'Thou shalt honour thy treaties'.[15]

Driven by this political-cultural criticism, the US Congress passed the American Indian Religious Freedom Act in 1978, which explicitly guaranteed the free exercise of religion for the Native American population. For Euro-Americans, this right had long been secured in the First Amendment, while Native Americans, as aforementioned, had previously been restricted by ritual prohibitions. This Act marked a reversal of the trend. But because place-based forms of spirituality were often related to land rights, the issue came under the competitive American judiciary. It was now courts that decided in costly lawsuits whether a religious practice was 'truly religious' and what this meant for land use. It turned out that the congressional decision often could not be enforced.[16]

However, one of the longest cases in American judicial history – lasting more than half a century – was decided in favour of the Native Americans, at least partially. In 1980, the Supreme Court ruled that the government's annexation of the Black Hills had violated the Fort Laramie Treaty of 1868 and should have been compensated. The court subsequently awarded the Lakotas and other Sioux groups over $100 million (estimated purchase value plus interest). But the Indians decided that they wanted the land back and did not want to sell it. This created a stalemate. The sum remained in the US Treasury and currently stands at well over $1 billion. As long as the money is not withdrawn, the claim to land has not been relinquished, so the Black Hills retain a kind of sanctity.[17]

Controversial Spirituality in National Parks

In addition to reservations for the Indigenous population, from the late nineteenth century onwards the United States established reservations for the tourist enjoyment of nature and later for actual nature conservation. Unlike the former category of land, the latter increased greatly in size in the twentieth century. A nationwide National Park Service was established to manage these designated areas. In global historical terms, the national park system is of considerable importance because it spread to many countries, especially after the Second World War. In the Black Hills area, the central government established the Devils Tower National Monument in 1906 and, after a series of other foundations, a Wilderness Area was established in the Black Hills Forest in 1980, named after the spiritual model Black Elk.[18]

According to research, the early national park movement was also based on quasi-religious motives. These are usually illustrated by the 'founding father' John Muir (1838–1914), a Scottish-American naturalist, much respected author and successful environmentalist. Muir broke away from a strict Calvinist background in his eventful life and developed a pantheistic philosophy of nature, which, however, often remained clothed in Christian language with an eye on the white readership. The *wilderness*, in the English Bibles the place of temptation – the equivalent of the *desert* (*Wüste*) in Luther's Bible – thus became a place of promise. Muir paid special attention to the mountains; on occasion he described his commitment as a conservationist as a 'Lord's battle' against the 'Prince of Darkness' who challenged the 'God of the Mountains'.[19]

The renewed and expanded ecological movement, which became part of the general critique of society and civilisation from the 1960s onwards, often drew on early conservationists such as John Muir. In addition, it took inspiration from Buddhist and other religious currents.[20] Particularly important now was the approach to Indigenous spirituality (which had remained alien to Muir's generation).[21] This was the time when Native Americans rose to become the ecological model in the politicised public sphere. The anthropocentric attitude of Christianity was held partly responsible for the serious environmental problems and contrasted with the Native Americans' reference to nature. As a result of this new connection, the national park authorities launched special programmes in which they used religious motifs for environmental education, as in the *Sacred Mountains Program* of 1998 (see Chapter 2).[22]

Some parks also imposed religiously motivated restrictions on use, which harboured considerable potential for conflict. At the aforementioned Devils Tower National Monument, northwest of the Black Hills, there were fierce conflicts between the group of rock climbers and the Native American communities, especially the Cheyenne. The latter used the site for Sun Dance ceremonies, prayer offerings and other rituals, but not for climbing. Among climbers, however, the spectacular, almost vertical 265-metre rock face is very popular. The sport is also accompanied by professional mountain guides. On the access road, however, the sportsmen have to take note of information boards: 'The Tower is Sacred to American Indians – Please Stay on Path'.[23]

In the 1990s, Native American complaints about this recreational activity increased. Under pressure from Cheyenne representatives, the National Park Service issued what was meant to be a compromise management plan in 1995: voluntary cessation of climbing in June, the peak period of religious-ceremonial use, accompanied by an education campaign about the spiritual significance of the site; suspension of guide licences for that month; no more climbing hooks; a ban on climbing routes that might disturb nesting hawks. In the first year of the compromise, most on both sides seemed reasonably satisfied. But several guides then formed an association and filed suit against the National Park Service for unrestricted access. They were supported by the powerful Mountain States Legal Foundation, which has emerged as an anti-environmentalist organisation since the 1970s and consistently denies Native American rights, even in cases where the Supreme Court has upheld the illegality of the US land annexation, as here.[24]

The climbing conflict also became a naming conflict. The Indigenous representatives felt that the registered name 'Devil's Tower' for their religious place was an insult and now wanted to officially give it the Indian name *Mato Tipi-la* (Bear Lodge), which is linked to a mythical origin story of the monolith. But in a 1996 vote, the community of 400 people to which the mountain belongs insisted on the 'white' name.[25] More successful was the Native Americans' campaign to rededicate the high Harney Peak in the Black Hills, named after a US general who commanded campaigns against their ancestors in the nineteenth century, one of which resulted in a massacre. After much debate, the US Board on Geographic Names decided in 2016 to rename it Black Elk Peak. A year later, the Roman Catholic diocese of the region even opened a petition to canonise the medicine man. So, his posthumous career does not seem to have come to an end. According to his biography, he was able to combine the Lakota faith with the Christian faith in an almost miraculous way. Should the petition come before the competent Congregation in Rome and finally before the Pope, I would be curious to hear the verdicts of these dignitaries as well as of the American people, regardless of their origins.[26]

~ 9 ~

VOLCANOES ON THE EAST AFRICAN RIFT VALLEY

The East African Rift extends from Djibouti for thousands of kilometres across the continent to Mozambique. The rift was formed by the drifting apart of two tectonic plates and continues to expand by a few millimetres per year. Associated with this rift is a high level of volcanic activity: there are many extinct, dormant or active volcanoes in the area. The most famous of these is Mount Kilimanjaro on the northern border of Tanzania, at 5,895 metres the highest mountain in Africa. No one who has ever seen its even shape rising from the plains, coming from the north or south, will ever forget the image.

The first European to report such an experience was the German Protestant missionary Johannes Rebmann. His caravan approached the mountains from the coast and came into sight-range on 11 May 1848. 'We saw the mountains of Dschagga more and more clearly this morning, by about 10 o'clock I thought I saw the summit of one of them, covered with a conspicuous white cloud.' The white patch turned out to be snow, which many geographers had thought impossible at this proximity to the equator. In the country itself, stories were heard that it was silver, and that it was an inaccessible mountain inhabited by evil spirits, an opinion the missionary was quick to explain away as the 'ignorance of the natives'. He himself picked up his Bible 'in the face of the magnificent snow mountain' and read Psalm 111: 'The works of the LORD are great, sought out of all them that have pleasure therein.' Rebmann was particularly touched by the sixth verse: 'He hath shewed his people the power of his works, that he may give them the heritage of the heathen.' What he had quietly suspected in this non-Christian environment, the verse expressed powerfully and clearly.[1]

The scene is characteristic of the problematic nature of this chapter. It remains unclear who exactly had which religious ideas about the volcanoes in the region. As the local language lacked a script, the views of the population are initially known only in the mirror of reports by Christian missionaries and other Europeans. This asymmetrical starting position is susceptible to extraneous attributions. Some foreigners brought with them an intense 'mountain faith' and were possibly anxious to endow the local people with one as well. So, anyone who finds research findings mostly in the negative to be meaningless would be better off skipping this chapter. For the general history of sacred mountains, however, such results are, in my opinion, of considerable interest, because they warn us against careless canonisations.

Searching for Clues on Mount Kilimanjaro

In the Kilimanjaro area, colonial supremacy originated from Germany during the 'Scramble for Africa'. Between 1885 and the First World War, it was part of German East Africa. Subsequently, the 'protectorate' was taken over by the British as the Tanganyika Territory.[2] Our first witness is Charles Dundas, a British colonial official who published an extended book on Kilimanjaro and its inhabitants in 1924. In the very first lines he gave free rein to his enthusiasm, proclaiming that those who live in the shadow of one of the most magnificent massifs on earth feel a spiritual attraction similar to the magnetic effect of large bodies on small ones. His enthusiasm was also that of a scientifically interested European mountaineer. He did not quite make it to the summit himself, but he paid tribute to those who had tried and succeeded (the first documented ascent was made by Hans Meyer and Ludwig Purtscheller in 1889). And he devoted himself to exploring the entire mountain area, which was populated by the Chagga or Dschagga people up to a sea level of about 2,000 metres. He ascribed to this local population a testimony that corresponded to his own attitude. For them, Kilimanjaro was 'the embodiment of all that is beautiful, eternal and strengthening'. The only bad omen is an unusually intense evening glow. It points to a coming famine.[3]

Did this 'embodiment' have a religious dimension? Dundas offers little evidence for this. The Chagga called their god Ruwa, which also meant sun. Whether the god was identical with the sun or the sun was the dwelling place of the god, they did not specify (in any case, it was not a mountain). Ruwa took little part in the lives of the people. But he was above all other forces and the final judge of fate.[4] According to Dundas, the locals were very reluctant to provide information about their religious practices. To find out more, he had hired a local helper. The mountain appeared in common sayings and some narratives. It also served as a landmark that provided ritual direction on certain occasions. The dead, for example, were buried with their faces facing the mountain. But there were no special religious occasions that turned to Kibo, as the mountain is called among the Chagga (this is generally the name for the highest volcanic cone).[5]

Two generations later, Edwin Bernbaum in California picked up Dundas' thread. In 1990, the religious scholar and alpinist described in Chapter 2 explicitly stated that Kilimanjaro was a sacred mountain, or at least had been in the past. The highest, most famous mountain in Africa thus confirmed his initial thesis of the general sacredness of mountains. But Bernbaum could not provide any more evidence for this than Dundas. In referring to the ritual orientation towards the summit, he surprised a student who had been educated in Christian schools in the Chagga region and studied at Berkeley in the 1980s. The American explained in detail to the African that there must have been a deeper meaning to it. Apparently, the latter was able to be convinced that 'many seemingly unimportant things in contemporary Chagga life', which he had never thought about, stemmed from ancient faith practices around the holy mountain.[6]

The literature on Kilimanjaro and Tanzania argues against this religion-laden interpretation. In an in-depth study of Chagga history from 1964, it is pointed out that Kibo plays an identity-creating role for the population at its foot. The mountain had nothing to do with magic or witchcraft, and the evil spirits reported by the missionary Rebmann were an invention of the people on the coast. They were not believed in locally. For religious practices, it was not the mountain that was important, but the shrines scattered in the agricultural area, mostly located in groups of trees.[7] The preliminary report and the decision of UNESCO, which inscribed Kilimanjaro National Park, founded in 1973, on the World Heritage List in 1987, point in the same direction. Local religious beliefs were generally respected by the organisation and used as a criterion. However, Kilimanjaro was only recognised for environmental reasons: because the mountain was a superlative natural phenomenon of exceptional natural beauty.[8]

At that time, historian John Iliffe was working on his classic history of Tanzania for the period from about 1800 until the country's secession from United Kingdom in 1961. It contains detailed chapters on the traditional religiosity of the different ethnic groups and on their changes. Prominent sacred mountains and relevant practices are not mentioned, but a colourful variety of 'nature spirits' is. Magical-religious rituals to summon rain were widespread in this mostly arid country. In the first place, however, Iliffe mentions a phenomenon that also often preoccupied the Christian missionaries with their monotheistic world view: most of the peoples in this East African country knew a single, supreme deity who appeared in various forms and ruled over the lower spirits.[9]

A Mountain of God by Hearsay

As we know from other sources, this supreme deity could also take up residence on a volcano, in particular places. An active volcano almost 3,000 metres high to the west of Kilimanjaro has become well known. The Maasai who inhabit the area call it Ol Doinyo Lengai, 'Mountain of God'.

A Mountain of God by Hearsay

The Maasai practised a semi-nomadic form of livestock farming in the vast plains of East Africa and were feared for their warlike behaviour and raids. Peaceful contacts with the Maasai were usually limited to caravan trade between the coast and the interior, trading ivory and slaves for cotton cloth, jewellery and firearms. An early account of the Maasai comes from Rebmann's partner, the German missionary Johann Ludwig Krapf. Krapf was a passionate linguist. A few weeks after arriving on the East African coast in 1844 and employing a Swahili teacher, he had already begun translating the Bible into this regional lingua franca. He attributed the problems in translating religious content to language deficiencies, not to the context, as one would do today: 'The languages of barbarian peoples are usually so poor that it is difficult in the beginning to find an adequate expression for the spiritual terms of the Bible, e.g. for justification, resurrection, saviour, holiness, etc.'[10]

In the 1850s, Krapf hired a man from the Wakuasi group (relatives or dependents of the Maasai) who had been sold away to the coast as a slave. From him he wanted to learn the language of the pastoralist population hundreds of kilometres away. From his stories, Krapf concluded that the Wakuasi and Maasai 'seem to have a faint idea of a supreme being whom they call Engai, which at first means "rain, sky". This supreme being dwells on the white mountain, whence comes the water or rain that is indispensable for their meadows and herds of cows.' There was also talk of pilgrimages of supplication which the shepherds made to the mountain and of prayers which they addressed to the god: 'Heaven (God), I beseech thee to let the land be clothed with grass.' Thus, they spoke and sang in a moving dance of prayer.[11] Where this event took place, however, remains unclear. The varying references to the place can be identified with several mountains – Ol Doinyo Lengai, the Mountain of God of the Maasai that appears in later writings, is not one of them.

Twenty-five years after Krapf, the German doctor and African explorer Gustav Adolf Fischer ventured into Maasai territory in person. On behalf of the Hamburg Geographical Society, he put together a 230-man caravan. In order not to appear European, he gave the people at the head a customary Islamic flag with verses from the Qu'ran. At the beginning of 1883, the column set out from the coast, and six months later it passed by the foot of Ol Doinyo Lengai without paying much attention to it. According to Fischer, religion was not very prominent among the Maasai. There were no ritual objects. Only the term *Ngai* seems to be linked to religious ideas. Before a war, people apparently ask this being for luck, and he heard the word often enough:

> When it thundered, they shouted 'ngai', the volcano they call Dönyo Ngai, when I launched my rockets, they shouted ngai, ngai, and many said ngai when they first saw me, especially when I lit matches. If you want, you can translate this word as 'God'. Anyway, the word is an expression for things that are inexplicable to them and seem to be a supernatural force.[12]

In 1917, the volcano Ol Doinyo Lengai erupted several times. The news received little attention for political reasons. The First World War was also being fought in East Africa at the time. Shortly afterwards, the British naturalist, big game hunter and author Thomas Alexander Barns climbed the slopes of this volcano during a Congo expedition. (His real target was a previously uncaptured species of butterfly in the Congo). According to his report, the Maasai considered the mountain sacred and the source of all blessings for their people. They interpreted the rumbling before the eruption as the roar of cattle that would soon come out and increase their wealth. After the eruption, they cordoned off the area, allowing only Maasai to enter. They brought in goats and cows, and women poured out the blood and milk of the cattle at the foot of the mountain. These two liquids had a high value in the diet of the Maasai. The mothers were also supposed to make an offering to the mountain god from their own breasts. Assuming that they would become pregnant, they were left there for a while. The Maasai refused to lead the Englishman up the volcano, which he attributed to the 'superstitious awe in which the "Mountain of God" is held by the Maasai'. He had to make the ascent himself with the porters he had brought with him.[13]

So Barns, too, knew the sacrificial rituals at Ol Doinyo Lengai only from hearsay, he had not seen them. At least his report shows a certain degree of detail. However, it can be assumed that it was a mountain of regional importance that appealed only to some sections of the Maasai. In the general literature on this well-known people, which has been traditionalist almost up to the present day, one looks for the mountain in vain.[14] Furthermore, we can assume that the religious history of Ol Doinyo Lengai did not begin before 1800 and was subject to various changes afterwards. The Maasai only migrated to this area at the beginning of the nineteenth century. Subsequently, their settlement area continued to expand before they were plunged into a crisis around 1890 – not least because of the German seizure of power. Under the British colonial administration, they were allocated special areas. At the same time, huge game reserves were created in the twentieth century. Today, the Mountain of God is located in the Loliondo Game Controlled Area, which adjoins the famous Ngornongoro Crater. Due to strict regulations, herders can only protect their herds from predators to a limited extent. In 1992, a luxury safari company from Dubai bought the right to hunt trophies here for millions.[15]

While Kilimanjaro experienced a huge rush of climbers and tourists in the second half of the twentieth century, Ol Doinyo Lengai has remained comparatively quiet. Various trekking companies advertise the Mountain of God, some emphasising only its attractive outer appearance, others also referring to its religious significance. Reinhold Messner stood on the volcano in October 1997 as part of the German television series *Abodes of the Gods* (see Chapter 1). Like his predecessors, he could only recount and explain the sanctity of the place from hearsay. One source was the Maasai guides who (unlike in the past) accompanied mountaineering tourists up the mountain and offered new versions of the stories that had been passed down. They did not give Messner the impression that they were afraid of a higher being.[16]

In general, as with Kilimanjaro, the world of the gods may not have weighed too heavily on this East African mountain – hardly to be compared with the ritual-religious conditions we encountered in Asia at the beginning of this book (Chapters 1–5). There was no shortage of nature spirits in Tanzania, according to John Iliffe, but they seem to have been less fond of mountains than the European mountaineers.[17]

~ 10 ~

AN INSELBERG IN THE AUSTRALIAN DESERT

Uluru or Ayers Rock is an inselberg in the central Australian desert, southwest of Alice Springs. Inselbergs are rock formations that rise abruptly from a flat landscape, making them highly visible and often attracting special attention. Uluru towers almost 350 metres above the desert. With its reddish sandstone, which takes on different colours in the course of the day, it has been a world-famous tourist attraction for some time now, despite its extreme remoteness, and merits comparison with higher, very famous mountains.

On 26 October 1985, over 3,000 people gathered at this site to 'return' Uluru to the Indigenous people, the Anangu Aborigines of that area, with a great celebration. Many had travelled hundreds or thousands of kilometres to pay their respects to the reinstated 'traditional owners'. Others had been showering the local group with letters of congratulations for days. It was clear to all that the object of the transfer was a sanctuary. For ten minutes, the celebration was disrupted by a small plane circling over the gathering with a banner attached and the words 'Ayers Rock for all Australians'. The banner was a reminder of the controversy that had roiled the country in previous months. In the course of it, some whites claimed that Ayers Rock was either not sacred at all, or vice versa: it was 'mystical' for everyone, including whites, and should not simply be surrendered. On this day, the black Aborigines felt victorious. Their hymn, written especially for the occasion, began with the words: 'We are the holder of many stories! Forever watch over great country.'[1]

The idea of the importance of possessing many stories and how this changed in the last 100 or 150 years will be discussed here. Because of the source situation in this culture without writing, it is difficult to go far back. We have arrived at a place that was settled for tens of thousands of years and then shaped by a highly uneven colonialism. When the British – and later other nations – flooded into the country from the late eighteenth century onwards, many saw the scattered ancient Indigenous population not as fellow human beings but as representatives of a Stone Age, in a sense of another universe.

'Stone Age' and 'Dreamtime'

'It was with no little relief and pleasure' that Baldwin Spencer caught sight of the inselberg in 1894 after a laborious journey through the arid landscape. 'Ayers Rock is probably one of the most striking objects in Central Australia', he wrote in his report. The British biologist, then a professor in Melbourne, took part in an expedition to explore this area, which was almost unknown to the white immigrant society. With much effort, he had brought along photographic equipment. The following day, the big rock was photographed for the first time ever (Figure 11). The most pressing problem for the expedition was water. A previous visitor had written that there were permanent waterholes here. Spencer's team found the claim exaggerated. In a dry season, it was better not to rely on it. In the evening, they climbed a little way up the rock walls. The mountain had only been climbed once before by a white man, who had named it after the politician Henry Ayers on that occasion in 1873. As Spencer looked down on the landscape, the 'desolate' area appeared to him brightened by the warm colours of the evening glow – a typical Australian desert, 'and to complete it as we looked down we saw a family of the native sandhill blacks making their way round the base of the mountain towards our camp'.[2]

Figure 11. Uluru or Ayers Rock in Central Australia in the first photograph, 1894.

The family consisted of a man, two women and several youths and children. They were apparently the only people staying there. They settled near the camp and Spencer and his translator spent the evening interviewing the man, 'our newly found friend, whose name was Lungkartitukukana'. According to Spencer, the family were among the 'lowest of the Australian Aborigines'. They were completely naked and their weapons and implements were of the simplest kind, almost without ornamentation. The stone tools had only been hewn and not polished and smoothed.[3] It is obvious that the explorer was fascinated by the 'genuinely wild state' of these people. When the expedition reached Alice Springs after about 350 kilometres, he met another soul mate. Francis James Gillen had spent two decades in this lonely area as an employee of the telegraph repeater station, turning his attention to the study of semi-mobile Aboriginal groups who subsisted on gathering and hunting. Together, Spencer and Gillen organised another expedition in the coming years and published their *Native Tribes of Central Australia* in 1899.[4]

The work immediately caused a stir in Western anthropology. Quite a few now used this message from the 'Stone Age' for their own purposes.[5] The Indigenous tribes made their most spectacular appearance via the French scholar Émile Durkheim, a co-founder of sociology. His 1912 book *The Elementary Forms of Religious Life* (*Les formes élémentaires de la vie religieuse*) was built primarily on the research of Spencer and Gillen. The book not only wanted to provide an analysis of their ethnography, but also an analysis of religion in general, which could be grasped here in its original form or essence.[6] Durkheim's treatise exerted a lasting influence on scholarship, but was also quickly met with scepticism and rejection. One knowledgeable critic (and devout Catholic) called it 'adventurous metaphysics' that neglected religious experience and selectively reproduced the descriptions of the two explorers.[7] For our topic of sacred mountains, the approach is indeed unhelpful. The sacred and the profane in a society are deductively derived and strictly separated in Durkheim's thought. His analysis is then primarily devoted to the rituals of the Aborigines and less to mythology.[8] But it was precisely in this that the 'holders of the stories' expressed their relationship to the landscape, and, when the land was overrun by immigrants, the stories, as we shall see, took on a completely different meaning.

The mythological narratives already had a prominent place with Spencer and Gillen. They also seem to have been the first to speak of 'dreams', and later the term 'dreamtime' became generally accepted. The Dreamtime is the formation phase of the world and extends into the present. Powerful ancestral beings travel the unformed earth and lead heroic, conflicted lives. Sometimes they transform into animals, terrain forms or natural phenomena such as fire, wind and rain. These ancestral journeys were memorised by Aboriginal males in chants lasting hours or even days. Geographically, they were tied to specific elements of the landscape, which were spread – conspicuously or inconspicuously – over large parts of central Australia. The entire region was covered by a matrix of living ancestral traces. Knowledge of these was acquired in gender-specific ways through songs and participation in rituals. The learning processes could last a lifetime, with old people often having especially much to tell.[9]

At Uluru, such narratives have been recorded in writing in various versions and at various levels of detail since the middle of the twentieth century. The stories only exceptionally concerned the inselberg as a whole. As a rule, they referred to individual sections and terrains. Charles P. Mountford, lover and populariser of Aboriginal rock art, described how the legends taught him to see the mountain with new eyes: learning of the snakes that fought around the Mutiguluna waterhole, the Marsupial rats and the desperate lizard with its lost boomerang helped him to see it in a new way. 'The immense and beautiful surroundings were no longer mere precipices, caves or splashes of colour; they had been vitalized by the stories that the aborigines had told me.'[10] It was by no means to be taken for granted that the author got to hear them at all, for parts of them were actually secret, and soon they were also to acquire a new economic value. The decisive factor was the change in white Australia.

From Ayers Rock to Uluru

In the interwar period, white settler Australia became a sovereign state within the British Empire, which transformed into the Commonwealth after the Second World War and gradually faded away. Parallel to the development in the industrialised West, the continent also experienced a transport revolution in the interwar period, with rapidly increasing motorisation, the onset of air travel and the further expansion of the railways. The large coastal cities, especially in the east, and the huge hinterland, the outback, thus moved closer together. Politics aimed in the same direction. Promoted by the federal government, the Australian National Travel Association (ANTA) was founded in 1929 with the mission of opening up the continent for tourism and thus stimulating a new patriotism. In the first phase, the organisation focused on the adventure romance of explorers and discoverers; later it profiled the spiritual culture of the Aborigines.[11]

The tourist strategies can be seen in the illustrated magazine *Walkabout*, which was published by the Secretary General of ANTA and reached a large readership. In the 1930s, for example, the magazine ran a series on 'The Unveiling of a Continent', which presented historical explorers and their heroic deeds. In 1941, a well-known travel writer was given the floor. He had recently joined an expedition to Ayers Rock. According to his report, the inselberg was considered 'the largest rock in the world' and represented a higher value than all the potential gold deposits the travel group wanted to explore. The long journey was made by plane, truck and camel. When the author finally saw the 'glories and beauties of Australia's Red Heart', he could even forget the strain of the camel ride. Arriving at his destination, he undertook a kind of reenactment of the first ascent in 1873, finding the cairn that marked the white occupation and writing his name on the list in the bottle housed there. For their exploration, the group needed a permit from the Department of the Interior, because the area had been a closed Aboriginal reserve since 1920.[12]

Nevertheless, some tourism began as early as the interwar period. After the war, 'the centre', as the area in the middle of the continent was increasingly called, also became a destination for organised educational trips. ANTA promoted 'Exploration Societies' at various schools from the late 1940s onwards, first for boys, later also for girls. Ayers Rock was soon to be one of the most distinguished destinations.[13] According to tourism historian Jillian Barnes, climbing the iconic rock became a rite of passage on the road to true Australianness:

> ANTA crafted Uluru into the training ground towards which prestigious schools and universities might direct Australia's future leaders to test themselves against the 'genius of the land', as well as to inspire the spirit of triumph and joy of discovery that had made a great white pioneering race.[14]

Barnes uses the concept of *sight sacralisation* and speaks of pilgrimages to a place that had taken on this sublime character thanks to the national founding generation.

Due to the strong increase in demand, the government took the inselberg and its surroundings out of the reserve in 1958 and assigned them to a newly created, public national park. The first ranger in charge of Uluru was William Harney. Unlike some of the early naturalists and tourists, he also had an interest in and a sympathy for the Aborigines. *Walkabout*, for example, published a text in which he compared the technical water search of the whites at Uluru with the astute local methods of the blacks, without pitting the two against each other.[15] In his five years as ranger, the number of visitors rose from a hundred to over 4,000 per year. At first, Harney was still able to cultivate his desert romance with visitors around nightly campfires, which contributed to his popularity in the country. To give the growing stream of visitors insights into the Dreamtime narratives of the Aborigines, he set up a circuit to certain mythological sites around the rock. In doing so, he created a whole new ritual that would eventually catch on.[16]

More and more, the Indigenous name Uluru came before Ayers Rock, although this white name remained common. As we have seen, the inselberg was officially 'returned' to the Aborigines in 1985. In the controversy surrounding this occasion, widespread ideas came to light. White Australians, according to their contributions to the discussion, did not feel they were tourists at Uluru. This type of visitor was stereotypically characterised in a negative way: tourists were profane, thoughtless, incapable of perceiving mysticism or spirituality, and many of them were Americans. White Australians, on the other hand, claimed an existential, moral right to Uluru. The difficult journey there and the climb up the Rock were described as proof of spiritual endurance. It was 'our biggest initiation ceremony'. Public talk about the sacred also took on a peculiarly stereotypical character in the controversy. What according to the official reading had traditional significance and sacredness among the Aborigines, was now regarded as unquestionable truth in the whole country. The best way to challenge the taboo was to postulate the rock's holiness 'for all Australians'.[17]

The Administration of the Sacred

An important reason for the standardisation of the sacred was the legal determination of Indigenous land rights. The Aborigines were in an awkward position vis-à-vis settlers, who claimed arid areas for grazing purposes, and mining companies, who were searching for mineral resources in many places. Their extensive land use, simple weapons and loose organisation were extremely unfavourable prerequisites for surviving in this tough, violent struggle. Soon, many migrated to the emerging white outposts (cattle ranches, missions, telegraph stations) and then to the distant towns. Their user rights were thus effectively lost. Similar to elsewhere, particularly the United States, a turning point in the relationship between the dominant immigrant society and the Indigenous population occurred around 1970. Politicians abandoned earlier ideas of assimilation and tended towards the doctrine of self-determination, which was, however, also imposed by the state and only partly negotiated in talks. It was also about reparation – more and more white Australians, in view of the immiseration of many Aborigines, felt that the country had incurred a moral debt and could not go on like this.[18]

The Northern Territory, where Uluru is located, was the testing ground for the new legislation. In 1976, the Aboriginal Land Rights Act was passed, followed by the Aboriginal Sacred Sites Act in 1989. With the first law, Aborigines could acquire a securitised title to certain areas, which henceforth belonged to them as inalienable property. To do so, they had to prove in court that they had 'traditional' ties to this land; among these, the 'spiritual' ones were of particular importance. The second law focused entirely on these spiritual or sacred places, which had meanwhile gained importance in social discourse. For their assessment, the judges used the testimonies of the Aborigines concerned (not least the Dreamtime narratives), the opinion of expert anthropologists and other circumstantial evidence.[19] At Uluru, the land application by the 'traditional owners' was fiercely contested by opponents, but eventually prevailed. For the Aborigines, this court case had the greatest practical and symbolic significance (hence the extensive 'return' celebration of 1985). In addition, the country was teeming with other sacred places. For the purpose of control and faithful administration, the authorities had to have public registers made of them. In the Northern Territory, hundreds of sacred sites have been recorded since 1989.[20]

Other efforts to reformulate the sacred involved rules to control the public. Certain narratives, rituals, places and images were reserved for initiated men among traditional Aborigines and were thus secret. Transgressions were sometimes punished by death. Popular and scholarly publications could undermine such prohibitions, which is why precautionary measures became commonplace. For example, in *Australian Aboriginal Religion*, published in the Netherlands in 1974, readers were urged to use the book in Aboriginal areas only after consultation with local religious leaders. When Charles P. Mountford, the aforementioned rock art expert, wanted to republish his 1965 book on Ayers Rock twelve years later, he had to omit two chapters.[21] There was also increasing pressure on museums to return ritual objects from Aboriginal areas to communities and individuals there, which usually proved difficult and was sometimes not welcome at all.[22]

At Uluru, religious arrangements have been an ongoing theme since the self-determination turn. In 1971, for example, the leader Paddy Uluru held a ceremony at the rock together with 25 elders. On this occasion, they showed the most sacred places to the chief ranger with the request to deny access to non-initiated tourists. In addition, information signs on misidentified 'dream sites' were to be removed.[23] In 2019, after lengthy discussions, the regulatory body, in which Aboriginal people were in the majority, issued a ban on climbing Uluru. The news was also taken as a symbolic message and went around the world: the most prominent white mountain ritual thus came to an end. The handrail chain that had supported so many visitors on the 350-metre climb since the 1960s was removed. The justification for the ban was, among other things, that there had been several sad deaths of tourists, and that the usual ascent path crossed an ancestral path from the Dreamtime.[24]

All in all, the inselberg in the Australian desert was a gauge of religious change. The traditional Aboriginal way of life, based on hunting and gathering activities, persisted in the Uluru area until the 1930s and was linked to a religious culture that attached mythological value to certain landscape elements. These dream places spread out in a network over wide areas. At Uluru, with its water points, they seem to have been condensed. In view of the low degree of centralisation of society, however, one should not overestimate the densification. White interest in the 'Red Heart of Australia' then promoted the focusing of perception on Uluru, and a generalisation to its entire iconic form rather than the specific story-points. National *sight sacralisation* enhanced the value of this particular Indigenous lore. Conceptually, the 'profane' tourists remained excluded in their notorious ignorance. The nationwide dynamics of self-determination that began around 1970 led to a new ritual order on the inselberg. Various overlays also emerged during this phase. For example, the Fusion Australia organisation has been organising annual Easter trips for young people since the turn of the millennium. 'Motivated by Christian values', it aims to promote transformation in individual lives and in community. At Uluru, young people have the opportunity to 'stop, listen and be transformed as they learn from the past, so they can change the future'.[25]

THE JOURNEY CONTINUES

~ 11 ~

WHAT FUTURE FOR SACRED MOUNTAINS?

Initiated primarily in the USA, an interdisciplinary research field of religion and ecology has been forming for several decades.[1] The new field lends itself particularly well as a framework for this concluding chapter on the development of the sacred mountains. It is itself an expression of a trend known as the 'Greening of Religion', which stems from the 'ecological turn' since around 1970. In the course of this, many religions took up ecological concerns and in turn formed a force encouraging further development in this direction. As far as Christianity is concerned, the trend is often illustrated with two high-profile texts: Lynn White's essay 'The historical roots of our ecologic crisis' as a critical prelude (1967) and Pope Francis' encyclical *Laudato si'* as a positive ecclesial response (2015).

The essay by the historian White was a warning shot that received a lot of attention because of its prominent place of publication, the journal *Science*. What was noted above all was the statement that the ecological crises increasingly perceived since the 1960s were due to religion: 'Especially in its Western form, Christianity is the most anthropocentric religion the world has seen.' Christianity had not only established a dualism of man and nature, but also insisted that it was God's will that humans should exploit nature for their own ends. With the rise of science, religion in the West had also taken on a technical character. Until the eighteenth century, scientific research had remained a religious endeavour, which had above all aspired to understand God's creation. In 1967, White placed his hope in the nature-oriented teachings of Saint Francis of Assisi. He was to be used as the patron saint of ecology.[2]

This spiritual protection for the environment was soon conceded by the Church, and a few decades later a Pope called himself Francis for the first time, presenting the saint as a model for the faithful and all humanity. The incipit title of the encyclical *Laudato si'* ('Praised be you') comes from the medieval religious founder's *Canticle of the Sun*. In 2015, Pope Francis and his many collaborators compiled an inventory of serious global environmental problems and commented on them from an ecclesial perspective. The encyclical went some way towards meeting critics like White. Instead of dualism, it speaks of the togetherness of all creatures; an 'integral ecology' deserves promotion. However, nature should not be deified, and the 'obsession with denying any pre-eminence to the human person' goes too far. Compared to previous church teaching, the cosmic hierarchy had become flatter, but otherwise remained untouched: God the Lord, then the human race and finally the rest of creation, to which one should relate 'as brothers and sisters'.[3]

If – inspired by the US researcher Bron Taylor – we further divide the green religions into colour levels, then Pope Francis' Catholicism forms a light green variant: nature as a 'sister', but not as a recognised sanctuary as in the dark green variants.[4] We could also place the colour change of Christianity in a long-term perspective. Then, for example, the aforementioned physico-theology of the seventeenth and eighteenth centuries should be mentioned. It gave greater weight to the 'book of nature' as opposed to the 'book of revelation' and thus already moved a step away from traditional anthropocentrism (Chapter 2). Here, however, I will try to reflect on the experiences from our site visits to sacred mountains around the globe and use these for an outlook on possible futures.

Religion and Environment, Globally

Mountains are very suitable as historical indicators for environmental perceptions and their change. Of course, a wide variety of elements attract human attention – rivers, lakes, trees, animals, clouds, winds, etc. On our Tour d'Horizon we indicated that mountains are often associated with other natural elements from a religious perspective. But their size and massiveness give prominence to mountains. Their exact shape also matters, but need not always play a decisive role: Sacred mountains can be difficult to take in as a whole, like the Pure Crystal Mountain in the rugged Tsari district of Tibet (Chapter 1), or emerge from a plain as iconic inselbergs, like Uluru in Australia (Chapter 10). Sometimes, too, it is not the mountains as a whole that are charged with religious significance, but individual sites and points. The following mountains have been treated in the order of their appearance in this book (continent, name, approximate date):

Asia: Tsari sixteenth–twentieth centuries
Kailash seventeenth–twenty-first centuries
Tai Shan eighth–twenty-first centuries
Paektusan thirteenth–twenty-first centuries

Europe: Alps nineteenth–twenty-first centuries;
Italian mountains around/after 1900

America: Black Hills nineteenth–twenty-first centuries

Africa: Kilimanjaro nineteenth–twenty-first centuries
Ol Doinyo Lengai nineteenth–twenty-first centuries

Australia: Uluru nineteenth–twenty-first centuries

The research journey touched almost every continent. The selection of examples was performed in a subjective way and mainly referred to well-known and significant mountains of the respective continents. Even with this makeshift method, the diversity of religious perception clearly emerged. The idea that all mountains in the world are, or once were, religiously significant, which has been propagated by various authors, cannot be substantiated. The idea that the sacredness of the mountains is primarily to be found in an early phase of history must also be problematised. In some cases, the extent of religious veneration increased massively during modern times; for example, in the case of Kailash in Tibet, which became a global model mountain of holiness in the twentieth century (Chapter 3).

The veneration was in stark contrast to traditional introverted Christianity, which paid little attention to the mountains. This gap in religious perception was filled during the early modern period by European nature research and subsequently by alpinism. Prompted by such 'modern' activities, the erection of summit crosses then led to a certain religious charge. It reached its ecclesiastical peak around or after 1900 (Chapters 6 and 7). The example of Kilimanjaro further shows that quite different forms of religiosity also managed without pronounced mountain references. Although we do not know whether the local population identified their main deity Ruwa with the sun or distinguished it from the sun, it was certainly not a mountain god, despite the majestic appearance of the African volcano (Chapter 9).

Due to the early development of writing, the sources on Asian and European mountains go back much further in time than those on the other continents, which are mainly based on the imported written form of the colonisers. Eurasian 'scripturalism' has been linked in a complex way with religious content and ideas of nature and mountains in an older research paper.[5] Here it seems more important to emphasise that the scope for specialisation of religious personnel was relatively closely linked to this mode of transmission. The connection was most conspicuously expressed in the monasteries, which devoted themselves entirely to traditional scripture and sometimes possessed large storehouses of printed material, as in Tibet. There could not have been so many religious specialists in oral societies. Writing and personnel increased the historical visibility of the sacred mountains and contributed to their widely perceived massing in Asia. The handwritten or printed guidebooks also facilitated pilgrimages (Chapters 1–5).

China had a strong affinity with a written culture associated with mountains. From the first millennium of our era, rocks were found in the empire that were covered with so-called *moya* stone inscriptions. During the modern era, these landscape inscriptions expanded further. For example, the listing of Tai Shan as a UNESCO World Heritage Site in 1987 was acknowledged by the prime minister with a cautionary rock calligraphy: 'Protect the world's heritage and establish the Eastern Sacred Peak'. Writing could also be used in a completely different way. The ages of regional or newly emerging deities were researched by the imperial Ministry of Rites using classical documents. For example, Bixia Yuanjun, the main female goddess on Tai Shan, gained a dubious reputation among Confucians because of a lack of evidence (Chapter 4).

Colonialism, Anti-Colonialism, 'Nature and Culture'

Very often, sacred mountains were, and are, about questions of identity for groups of different sizes, up to nations and beyond. This dimension was reinforced by colonialism and imperialism, both European-American and Asian, which became rampant in modern times. An extreme colonialism effect can be grasped at Paektusan on the Korean-Chinese border. A Buddhist story written down in the thirteenth century told of the miraculously begotten mountain figure Tangun. The figure only became a broadly revered progenitor of Korea through the fierce national defensive struggle against Japanese colonialism in the early twentieth century. Later, the Kim dictatorship in North Korea added its own myths to the mountain and made it the 'sacred mountain of the revolution' (Chapter 5).

In the Black Hills in the Midwest of the USA, the colonial confrontation found a material expression, carved in stone. The immigrant Euro-Americans met the Lakota Sioux here in the nineteenth century. In order to culturally profile the victorious 'Pax Americana' and its civil-religious ideas, a large sculpture was created, initially against Christian objections. Four superhuman US presidents have looked down from Mount Rushmore since the 1940s. In response, advocates of the Native American cause began to carve a large-scale figure of a leader out of another peak's rock (Chapter 8).

Around 1970, the political-cultural balance of power shifted. Criticism of modern industrial society, with its ecological problems and military entangle-

Colonialism, Anti-Colonialism, 'Nature and Culture'

ments, increased by leaps and bounds; the Native American self-determination movement gained strength, and its spirituality was now highly regarded by a section of white Americans (instead of being considered un-Christian or non-existent as before). We found a parallel development among the Aborigines in Australia at Uluru (Chapter 10). These shifts in power were in the context of global decolonisation, and with them the debate about 'nature and culture' also changed, having first been used as an intellectual weapon by the West from the nineteenth century onwards. Contrary to what one often hears, the pairing of these terms is historically young and by no means the product of a twin birth. In European scholarly language, 'nature' looks back on a much older history than 'culture'. The latter expression was, among other things, a parallel term to 'civilisation' and served as a European brand of superiority during colonial expansion.[6]

In the religious sphere, the inferiority of the other societies was also expressed biblically. The German missionary who was the first to report from Kilimanjaro in the middle of the nineteenth century (Chapter 9) said about Africa: 'The deep apostasy of man from God is also shown in these countries in that nature rules over him instead of he over nature.'[7] Similar ideas were conveyed by the concept of nature for more than a hundred years. For example, a study first published in 1951, which continued and renewed the European tradition of great philosophy, found the following words about the African population:

> What made them different from other human beings was not at all the color of their skin but the fact that they behaved like a part of nature, that they treated nature as their undisputed master, that they had not created a human world, a human reality, and that therefore nature had remained, in all its majesty, the only overwhelming reality – compared to which they appeared to be phantoms, unreal and ghostlike.[8]

When the anti-colonial and Indigenous movements gained strength after 1960 and the Western-Christian views went on the defensive, the tide turned. The conceptual pair nature–culture now became a handicap because it was seen as an expression of a dualistic rather than a holistic worldview. The 'separation from nature' developed into a much-discussed topic and sometimes into the main characteristic of European history. This is the case with the French anthropologist Philippe Descola, who positions the small societies he studied in the Amazon and elsewhere *Beyond Nature and Culture* (*Par-delà nature et culture*), as the title of his 2005 book announces.[9] In fact, the pair of opposites proves to be of little use in the global context, but its empirical viability should not be overestimated for Europe either: in fact, the purported 'great divide of nature and culture', created by early modern scientific research, remains unclear. For a balanced assessment, one should not limit oneself to the narrow history of science and philosophy, but also question the history of religion and social history. This would show that the majority of European anthropocentrism was of ancient, Christian origin.[10]

Pope Francis' environmental encyclical from 2015, mentioned at the beginning of this chapter, can be read as the Church's response to this postcolonial holistic offensive. It pursued a double strategy. On the one hand, it promoted an authentically lived 'integral ecology'; on the other, it shifted the accusation of anthropocentrism from faith to the faithful. The latter should show more humility and not place themselves too much in the centre.[11]

Social Roles

While mountains serve as indicators for environmental perceptions, gender roles on the mountain can contribute to a deeper understanding of societies. On the Pure Crystal Mountain in Tibet (Chapter 1), the higher circumambulation routes were reserved for men, and women had to make do with the lower ones. There was a relationship between ritual rank and religious space: the low-outer zone was open to women, the middle-inner zone to all men and the high-central/inner zone only to the spiritually advanced, 'pure' men. The Crystal Mountain belonged to the highly sacred mountains with a supra-regional and potentially dangerous aura. In the local mountain cults, the exclusion of women went even further: they could not participate. It is assumed that the Tantric practitioners took up this local exclusion and partially transformed it. Tibetan Buddhism's belief in women's low birth rank and impurity also played a significant role. In 1959, Communist China banned all pilgrimages. When the authorities allowed them again in 1984, the locals again relied on the gender hierarchy – not without resistance from some women.[12]

More generally, male primacy at sacred mountains has often been ritually emphasised, in Tibet and the rest of Asia as well as on other continents. The distribution of roles points to their deep roots in the dominating patriarchal societies and may prove to be a handicap for the future of such forms of mountain worship. However, it could also be an opportunity for women (and other genders or non-genders) to rediscover and claim symbolic places for themselves. Historical and contemporary examples suggest that this change could be quite varied.

The much-visited Fujiyama in Japan, known as the national mountain, is well documented and studied. It has been venerated by mountain ascetics

Social Roles

of various doctrines since the Middle Ages. From the late fifteenth century onwards, pilgrimage to the mountain increased sharply. Parallel to the more and more rigorous exclusion of women, the practice started to receive criticism, first from genuinely religious currents. The ascetic Jikigyo Miroku, who starved himself to death on the mountain in 1733 and became a celebrity, stated: 'A woman cannot be sinful if she does nothing wrong.' A successor expanded the gender theology, striving for a harmonious relationship between *yin* and *yang* and also giving advice on the nature of sexual intercourse. Later, members of this current moved on to symbolic actions. In 1832, a woman secretly reached the forbidden summit of Fujiyama. The increasing relaxation of the ban on women was also due to economic competition between the operators of the various access routes, who lived off the pilgrimage and strove to develop it. In 1860, the ban was temporarily lifted, and in 1872 the volcano was opened to both sexes. Special circumstances connected with the Meiji Revolution contributed to this. The fact that the deities of Fujiyama were more significant to the lower classes than to the ruling ones was also important.[13]

The situation is quite different on the Holy Mountain of Athos, where the Christian Orthodox monks still maintain the exclusion of women from their peninsula. We know that the ecclesiastical-religious presence on Mount Athos was holier than the mountain itself; its meaning is to be understood very metaphorically (Chapter 6). But this very fact may have contributed to the stubborn defence of the exclusion. It is said to apply here even to the animal world. Particularly since Greece's membership of the European Community/Union, controversy has arisen time and again. In 2003, the European Parliament called for the mountain's release in a non-binding decision. Greece, it said, should lift the threat of several months' imprisonment for transgression. The Parliament stated that 'such a ban is a violation of the principle of and the international conventions on gender equality and non-discrimination on the basis of gender and the provisions relating to free movement of persons provided by the Greek Constitution and Community law'.[14]

The monks on Athos also pursue a special strategy in another social role assignment: the mountain is only accessible to pilgrims, not tourists. Regardless of their origin, orientation and motivation, all male visitors officially transform themselves into 'pilgrims'. Compulsory registration allows the flow of visitors to be controlled; there is an upper limit and rules regarding the length of stay are enforced.[15] The distinction between pilgrimage and tourism is thus also set by the leading protagonists themselves. One encounters such sweeping categorisations in many places and in very different forms. When Chinese literati visited the sacred mountains of the early modern empire, they programmatically distinguished themselves from the pilgrims of the lower classes, whom they liked to call superstitious (Chapter 2).[16] When tourism at Uluru/Ayers Rock in Australia began to take off in the 1960s, a section of white Australians did not want to be considered tourists: for them, the 'Red Heart of Australia' represented a spiritual-national test. Tourists were of a different, inferior quality in their eyes, namely ignorant, materialistic foreigners (Chapter 10).

In recent decades, both specialised tourism studies and pilgrimage studies have experienced an international upsurge. Studies in these fields emphasise the overlaps between the two broadly defined forms of mobility. The term pilgrim consolidated in Europe during the seventeenth century and is usually associated with religious institutions. The term tourist emerged in the nineteenth century, when the modern transport revolution began. Today, however, researchers also speak of religious tourism and of secular pilgrimages or the sacralisation of tourist sites (*sight sacralisation*).[17] The emphasis is on frameworks and behaviours that link the two fields. Of course, one can ask whether this use of language is not too broad and transposed. But I do not believe that a general answer can be found. In order to make a proper decision, we should above all pay attention to the statements and behaviours of the actors on the ground (see below).

In this context, it can also be asked whether there were quantitatively certain points of transition from sacred to profane in the history of mountains and what this might mean for the future. From Asian examples referred to in this book, it appears that a small number of spiritual mountain pioneers were often followed after some time by large, popular pilgrimages, which may have jeopardised earlier forms of veneration (Chapters 1, 3 and 11). Heroic loners can easily give the impression of deep, extraordinary holiness, while mass pilgrims may exude something mundane and attract profane tourists. For the future, this could mean that the sacredness of the mountains would have to be set in motion again and again in new places, because the old places would be subject to a regular process of secularisation. But there are also reasons that speak against this simple scheme. To name just one: the idea of a deep, because lonely, religiosity in the mountains could be brought about above all by our romantic ideas. We know of many mass religious events around the world that are considered entirely sacred.[18]

Environmental and Climate Protection

With the ecological turn around 1970, the older idea of 'nature conservation' was conceptually overlaid by 'environmental protection', which a generation later had to give way – to some extent – to 'climate protection'. In the heyday of environmentalism, a strategic link between Western ecologists and Indigenous societies emerged. In the eyes of many critics of modern industrial society, other cultures showed that it was also possible to treat the environment in a considerate and sustainable way (Chapter 8). Since the sacredness of natural elements formed a potential protective factor, and Indigenous people mostly seemed to be responsible for the sacred, possible alliances of interest emerged. A number of projects therefore explored how sacred mountains, for example, could be used for environmental protection.

In the 1990s, the International Union for Conservation of Nature (IUCN) took a corresponding initiative at the global level. It set up a working group on the 'cultural and spiritual values of protected areas'. After several international conferences, the group took stock at an event in Barcelona in 2008. Eight 'guardians' of Sacred Natural Sites from four continents were invited: Asia, Latin America, Africa and Australia/Oceania (while the organisers and funders were from Europe and North America). In conclusion, the organisers argued that sacred natural sites should be recognised as the first network of protected areas in history, much older than the modern nature and national parks that have emerged since the late nineteenth century. These time-honoured sites make an important contribution to the preservation of biodiversity. Tourism could benefit them economically, but it could also pose a cultural and ecological threat. The major religions were described as 'mainstream religions' (not 'world religions' as they liked to see themselves). Conspicuously absent among them was Islam, perhaps because it was a geopolitical hot issue. At the very least, Indigenous religions seemed more suitable for conservation than the religious mainstream.[19]

Accordingly, their representatives were brought to the fore. The preface of the conference publication featured a long poem written for the occasion by a Siberian shaman about her sacred mountain Alkhanai, beginning with an admonition to its visitors ('What are you tourists doing, so-called pilgrims?'). At the end, the representatives were able to make their own statement, which can be understood as a global Indigenous doctrine. What strikes us about it is the wide extension of sacredness:

> We also note that for many of us our whole territories are sacred and this includes our homes, communities, farms, footpaths, markets and meeting places; and that these territories include layers of sacredness often with different purposes, including those that are material and functional to humans.[20]

What Future for Sacred Mountains?

Just as conservationists began to form a picture of Indigenous peoples, so the latter began to form a picture of ecology and its claims. This 'reverse environmentalism' is well studied among Tibetan Buddhists in China. From the end of the twentieth century, a network of non-governmental organisations spread in the highlands. The age of projects began. At the sacred mountain Khawakarbo, for example, the number of visitors had increased massively, which affected the local incense cypress. These trees provide a habitat for small animals, help improve the climate and reduce soil erosion. Thanks to an ecological project, incense consumption was greatly reduced. Central to this was the teaching of two monks who questioned the karmic merit of pilgrims who burned 'the very best ornaments' of the mountain as an offering.[21] Some Tibetan activists, however, perceived the Western environmentalists as arrogant, not only because they had the money and thus ultimately the say, but also for religious reasons. Presuming that they had the power to protect the environment was, in their eyes, a presumptuous, self-righteous belief; its condition depended more on the inner state of mind on the Buddha's path than on external actions. And the concept of biodiversity, which places a higher value on rare species, was deemed unfair; all sentient beings in the world deserved the same care and mindfulness.[22]

Critical scholars of religion have also raised the question of whether and to what extent religious beliefs of any kind contribute to environmental protection at all. The question is complex and difficult to answer empirically. The authors therefore resort to opinion research. They processed hundreds of scholarly articles in the field and came to an ambivalent conclusion: religions do indeed matter for ideational and practical attitudes towards the environment, but the ongoing process of the 'Greening of Religions' is driven far more by social forces than by intra-religious ones.[23] This supports the idea that the alliance of (secular) environmentalism and (Indigenous) religion regarding sacred mountains could continue to be important in the future. On the part of global politics, however, a relative decrease in backing is possible. The tendential shift from biodiversity to CO_2-reduction as a means against global warming – i.e. the focus on climate policy – leads away from terrestrial to atmospheric realms. Even sacred mountains, however, remain mostly terrestrial.

Mount Sacred – The Twenty-first Century

In the early twentieth century, two pioneers of Western sociology dealt with religious issues in a global, intercultural way. Émile Durkheim, in his *The Elementary Forms of Religious Life*, chose the Aborigines of Australia as a starting point (Chapter 10). In 1920, the year of Max Weber's death, his *Collected*

Mount Sacred – The Twenty-first Century

Essays on the Sociology of Religion (*Gesammelte Aufsätze zur Religionssoziologie*) were published, dealing with the economic ethics of faiths and containing, for example, many remarks on China. Neither of these foundational works dealt in depth with the relationship between religion and nature,[24] but they had a strong influence on later attempts to define religious phenomena scientifically. Today, there are two classical types of definitions of 'religion' to choose from: substantive ones, which, for example, interpret belief in spiritual beings as a basic characteristic; and structural-functionalist ones, which consider general effects on society (such as integration into a moral community). In addition, since the late twentieth century, another form has become established that appeals to the 'family resemblance' of the religious and leaves the boundaries to profane phenomena relatively open and determined by the actors themselves. In his study of the 'dark green' environmental religious currents of the present, Bron Taylor, for example, has resorted to this approach.[25]

For the present book, I decided on this open variant for several reasons. The most important seemed to me to be the fact that the level of discourse, which is relatively neglected in the classical definitions, plays a central role for the topic of sacred mountains. Who can express themselves more competently about a certain form of sacredness than the people directly or also indirectly involved in the event? In the process, it becomes apparent that individual opinions also diverge and, under certain circumstances, lead to considerable fluctuations in public opinion.

The treatment of the mountains by the French Revolution is an example of this. Against the background of the new importance of nature in European science and culture, there was a strong politicisation of nature at that time. It produced a kind of sacred mountains – symbolic, extra-religious and as a passing fashion. For reasons that are not entirely clear, some of the revolutionaries identified with the mountains. They went by the name 'mountain people' (*montagnards*) and used artificially created mountains as embodiments of nature for their newly conceived political rituals. In 1793 and 1794, during the most violent phase of the revolution, the cult reached its peak. Shortly afterwards, the mountain *coulisses* were described in the National Convention as 'monuments of terror'. One deputy said that he could see in the mountains a symbol of the people, but that they were also a cause of division: 'A mountain, is it not an eternal revolt against equality?' So the Convention decided to abolish all artificial mountains in the Republic (Chapter 1).

The politicisation of nature before and during the French Revolution had a different character from the politicisation of the environment that we have experienced in recent decades. The industrial upheavals of modernity were in their infancy then. People still intervened far less in environmental events than they do today. But the example shows how much we depend on path-dependent developments when predicting the future. Before the onset of the revolution, no one could really foresee that the usual course of events would soon lead to an upheaval of such explosive force and global impact, keeping society on tenterhooks for years. Anyone who wants to look from the past into the future must be aware that, apart from manageable historical forces, there are many contextual forces that we cannot know in advance.

As indicated several times in this concluding chapter, the prospects for *Mount Sacred* have a mixed record. At play are numerous forces with complex effects: colonialism, anti-colonialism and indigeneity, gender, tourism, environmentalism, to name only the most important. Assuming that neither a secular nor a religious groundswell sweeps the entire mountain world in the next few generations, I suspect that the question of the future is better answered on an individual scale – as predictions for particular cases. From Mount Kailash in Tibet to the Black Hills in South Dakota to Uluru in the Australian desert, the history of sacred mountains has been strongly marked by diversity. In the middle and at the end of the twenty-first century, it could continue to be of considerable importance. Such a presumption of diversity would also suit the faithful, many of whom like to think of their shrines as unique rather than, as they say in the Far East, *mountains beyond mountains*: there are mountains beyond mountains, but only one or a few touch us. Would it be better if, in the future, they were all alike?

SELECT BIBLIOGRAPHY

Here I list the publications cited several times; all others are reported in the endnotes.

Barnes, Jillian. 'Tourism's role in the struggle for the intellectual and material possession of "The Centre" of Australia at Uluru (Ayers Rock), 1929–2011', *Journal of Tourism History* 3/2 (2011): 147–76.
Bernbaum, Edwin. *Sacred Mountains of the World*. Berkeley, 1997 (revised edition: Cambridge 2022).
Bernbaum, Edwin. 'Sacred Mountains: Themes and Teachings', *Mountain Research and Development* 26/4 (2006): 304–09.
Bingenheimer, Marcus. 'Pilgrimage in China'. In Dionigi Albera and John Eade (eds.), *New Pathways in Pilgrimage Studies. Global Perspectives*. New York, 2017, pp. 18–35.
Boscani Leoni, Simona (ed.) *'Unglaubliche Bergwunder'. Johann Jakob Scheuchzer und Graubünden. Ausgewählte Briefe 1699–1707*. Chur, 2019.
Brown, Peter. *The Making of Late Antiquity*. Cambridge MA, 1978.
Chavannes, Edouard. *Le T'ai Chan. Essai de monographie d'un culte chinois*. Paris, 1910.
Coster, Will and Andrew Spicer (eds.). *Sacred Space in Early Modern Europe*. Cambridge, 2005.
Dundas, Charles. *Kilimanjaro and its People. A History of the Wachagga, their Laws, Customs and Legends, together with Some Account of the Highest Mountain in Africa*. London, 1924.
Das heilige, allgültige und allgemeine Concilium von Trient, das ist: dessen Beschlüsse und hl. Canones nebst den betreffenden päpstlichen Bullen treu übersezt von Jodoc. Egli. Grätz, 1827.
DeMallie, Raymond J. (ed.) *The Sixth Grandfather. Black Elk's Teachings Given to John G. Neihardt*. Lincoln, 1984.
Dott, Brian R. *Identity Reflections. Pilgrimages to Mount Tai in Later Imperial China*. Cambridge MA, 2004.
Dott, Brian R. 'Spirit Money. Tourism and Pilgrimage on the Sacred Slopes of Mount Tai'. In Tim Oakes and Donald S. Sutton (eds.) *Faiths on Display. Religion, Tourism, and the Chinese State*. Lanham, 2010, pp. 27–50.
Durkheim, Émile. *Les formes élémentaires de la vie religieuse. Le système totémique en Australie*. Paris, 1912.
Elliott, Mark C. 'The Limits of Tartary: Manchuria in Imperial and National Geographies'. *The Journal of Asian Studies* 59/3 (2000): 603–46.
Fabrini, Natale. *Il Conte Giovanni Acquaderni*. Bologna, 1991 (first published 1945).

Select Bibliography

Fischer, Gustav A. 'Bericht über die im Auftrage der Geographischen Gesellschaft in Hamburg unternommene Reise in das Massai-Land'. In *Mittheilungen der Geographischen Gesellschaft in Hamburg, Jg. 1882–83*. Hamburg, 1883–84, pp. 36–99, 189–237.

Francis (Pope). *Encyclical Letter* Laudato si'. *On Care for Our Common Home*. Vatican, 2015.

Gantke, Wolfgang. *Der umstrittene Begriff des Heiligen. Eine problemorientierte religionswissenschaftliche Untersuchung*. Marburg, 1998.

Gaspari, Oscar. 'Il Giubileo del 1900 nelle montagne italiane: spiritualità, politica e alpinismo'. *Storia e Futuro* 53 (February 2021): www.storiaefuturo.eu (accessed 8 March 2021).

Govinda, Anagarika. *The Way of the White Clouds. A Buddhist Pilgrim in Tibet*. London, 1966.

Gratzl, Karl (ed.) *Die heiligsten Berge der Welt*. Graz, 1990.

Grayson, James H. 'Tan'gun and Chumong: The Politics of Korean Foundation Myths'. *Folklore* **126**/3 (2015): 253–65.

Harrist, Robert E. *The Landscape of Words. Stone Inscriptions from Early and Medieval China*. Seattle, 2008.

Huber, Toni. *The Cult of Pure Crystal Mountain. Popular Pilgrimage and Visionary Landscape in Southeast Tibet*. Oxford, 1999.

Huber, Toni. 'Putting the Gnas Back into Gnas-skor: Rethinking Tibetan Buddhist Pilgrimage Practice'. In idem (ed.) *Sacred Spaces and Powerful Places in Tibetan Culture. A collection of Essays*. Dharamsala, 1999 (quoted as 1999b), pp. 23–60.

Jenkins, Willis et al. (eds.). *Routledge Handbook of Religion and Ecology*. Abingdon, 2017.

Kasper, Michael and Robert Rollinger (eds.). *Religion in den Bergen* (Montafoner Gipfeltreffen, Bd. 5). Vienna, forthcoming (2023).

Kim il-sung. *Reminiscences: With the Century*, 8 vols. Pyongyang, 1993–2007.

Kouamé, Natalie and Vincent Goossaert. 'Un vandalisme d'état en Extrême-Orient? Les destructions de lieux de culte dans l'histoire de la Chine et du Japon'. Numen 53/2 (2006): 177–220.

Krapf, Johann Ludwig. *Reisen in Ostafrika, ausgeführt in den Jahren 1837–1855*, newly edited with an introduction by Hanno Beck. Stuttgart, 1964.

Kunz, Wolfgang. *Gipfelkreuze in Tirol. Eine Kulturgeschichte mit Gegenwartsbezug*. Vienna, 2012.

Lammer, Eugen Guido. *Durst nach Todesgefahr*, ed. by Reinhold Messner and Horst Höfler. Augsburg, 1999.

Landt, Frank A. *Die fünf Heiligen Berge Chinas. Ihre Bedeutung und Bewertung in der Ch'ing Dynastie*. Berlin. 1994.

Layton, Robert. *Uluru. An Aboriginal History of Ayers Rock*. Canberra, 1986.

Larner, Jesse. *Mount Rushmore. An Icon Reconsidered*. New York, 2002.

Lim, Jae-Cheon. *Leader Symbols and Personality Cult in North Korea: The Leader State*. London, 2015.

Löwer, Hans-Joachim. *Gipfelkreuze. Träume, Triumpfe, Tragödien*. Innsbruck, 2019.

Mathieu, Jon. *The Third Dimension. A Comparative History of Mountains in the Modern Era*. Cambridge, 2011.

Select Bibliography

Mathieu, Jon. *Die Alpen. Raum – Kultur – Geschichte*. Stuttgart, 2015.

Mathieu, Jon. 'Der heilige Berg der Revolution'. In Alpines Museum der Schweiz (ed.) *Let's Talk About Mountains* (Begleitpublikation zur Nordkorea-Ausstellung). Bern, 2020, pp. 114–21.

McKay, Alex. *Kailas Histories. Renunciate Traditions and the Construction of Himalayan Sacred Geography*. Leiden, 2015.

McKay, Alex. 'The British Imperial Influence on the Kailas-Manasarovar Pilgrimage'. In Toni Huber (ed.) *Sacred Spaces and Powerful Places in Tibetan Culture. A Collection of Essays*. Dharamsala, 1999, pp. 305–21.

Messner, Reinhold and Ralf-Peter Märtin. *Meine heiligen Berge*. Berlin, 2013.

Miller, Mary Ashburn. *A Natural History of Revolution. Violence and Nature in the French Revolutionary Imagination, 1789–1794*. Ithaca, 2011.

Mills, Kenneth. *Idolatry and its Enemies. Colonial Andean Religion and Extirpation, 1640–1750*. Princeton, 1997.

O'Malley, John W. *Trent. What Happened at the Council*. Cambridge MA, 2013.

Osterhammel, Jürgen. *Die Verwandlung der Welt. Eine Geschichte des 19. Jahrhunderts*. München, 2011.

Ostler, Jeffrey. *The Lakotas and the Black Hills. The Struggle for Sacred Ground*. New York, 2010.

Pomeranz, Kenneth. 'Power, Gender, and Pluralism in the Cult of the Goddess of Taishan'. In Theodore Huters et al. (eds.). *Culture and State in Chinese History. Conventions, Accommodations, and Critiques*. Stanford, 1997, pp. 182–204.

Rime, Jacques. *Le baptême de la montagne. Préalpes fribourgeoises et construction religieuse du territoire (XVIIe–XXe siècles)*. Neuchâtel, 2021.

Robson, James. *Power of Place. The Religious Landscape of the Southern Sacred Peak (Nanyue) in Medieval China*. Cambridge MA, 2009.

Scharfe, Martin. *Berg-Sucht. Eine Kulturgeschichte des frühen Alpinismus 1750–1850*. Vienna, 2007.

Speake, Graham. *A History of the Athonite Commonwealth. The Spiritual and Cultural Diaspora of Mount Athos*. Cambridge, 2018.

Spencer, Baldwin. *Report on the Work of the Horn Scientific Expedition to Central Australia*. London, 1896.

Stahl, Kathleen M. *History of the Chagga People of Kilimanjaro*. London, 1964.

Stutfield, Hugh E.M. 'Mountaineering as a Religion'. *The Alpine Journal* 32 (1918–1919): 241–47.

Suh, Dae-Sook. *Kim il Sung: The North Korean Leader*. New York, 1988.

Sulzer, Johann Georg (ed.) *Johann Jacob Scheuchzers Natur-Geschichten des Schweizerlandes, samt seinen Reisen über die Schweitzerische Gebürge*. Zurich, 1746.

Taylor, Bron. *Dark Green Religion: Nature Spirituality and the Planetary Future*. Berkeley, 2010.

Select Bibliography

Thomas, Keith. *Man and the Natural World. Changing Attitudes in England 1500–1800.* New York, 1983.

Tichy, Herbert. *Zum heiligsten Berg der Welt. Auf Landstrassen und Pilgerfahrten in Afghanistan, Indien und Tibet.* Vienna, 1937.

Trepp, Anne-Charlott. *Von der Glückseligkeit alles zu wissen. Die Erforschung der Natur als religiöse Praxis in der Frühen Neuzeit.* Frankfurt a. M. 2009.

Verschuuren, Bas et al. (eds.). *Sacred Natural Sites. Conserving Nature and Culture.* London, 2010.

Whittacker, Elvi. 'Public Discourse on Sacredness: The Transfer of Ayers Rock to Aboriginal Ownership'. *American Ethnologist* 21/2 (1994): 310–34.

Xueqin, Mei and Jon Mathieu. 'Mountains Beyond Mountains: Cross-Cultural Reflections on China'. Marcus Hall and Patrick Kupper (eds.). *Crossing Mountains. The Challenges of Doing Environmental History* (Rachel Carson Perspectives 2014/4). Munich, 2014, pp. 31–41.

Yeh, Emily T. 'Reverse Environmentalism. Contemporary Articulations of Tibetan Culture, Buddhism and Environmental Protection'. In James Miller et al. (eds.). *Religion and Ecological Sustainability in China.* Abingdon, 2014, pp. 194–219.

Zedler, Johann-Heinrich (ed.) *Grosses vollständiges Universal-Lexicon aller Wissenschaften und Künste,* 64 vols. and Supplemente. Halle/Leipzig, 1732–1752.

Zwyssig, Philipp. *Täler voller Wunder. Eine katholische Verflechtungsgeschichte der Drei Bünde und des Veltlins (17. und 18. Jahrhundert).* Affalterbach, 2018.

NOTES

Writings cited more than once appear in the bibliography and are usually identified in the endnotes in an abbreviated manner (author, year, page).

Foreword

1. Hindustan Times, Chandigarh Edition on 17 Feb. 2006; for the historical background, see Chetan Singh, 'Long-Term Dynamics of Geography, Religion, and Politics. A Case Study of Kumharsain in the Himachal Himalaya', *Mountain Research and Development* 26/4 (2006): 328–35 and Chetan Singh, *Himalayan Histories. Economy, Polity, Religious Tradition* (Albany NY, 2018).
2. There are many dimensions of 'nature'; this book focuses on the landscape aspects.
3. Similar to Christianity, mountains played a relatively minor role in learned Islamic cosmology, which does not preclude the possibility of their being significant in regional popular traditions (for example as burial sites); see the chapter by Stephan Prochazka in Kasper and Rollinger 2023; on the issue of Islamic anthropocentrism, see Zainal Abidin Bagir and Najiyah Martiam, 'Islam. Norms and practices', in Jenkins 2017, pp. 79–87.
4. Peter H. Hansen, *The Summits of Modern Man. Mountaineering after the Enlightenment* (Cambridge MA, 2013); Jon Mathieu, 'Globalisation of Alpinism in the Twentieth Century: Publicity, Politics, and Organisational Endeavours', *Comparativ. Zeitschrift für Globalgeschichte und vergleichende Gesellschaftsforschung* 30/3–4 (2020): 410–22.
5. Luigi Corvi, 'Buddha o croce, la sfida in vetta', Corriere della Sera 9 Sept. 2005; see chapters 3 and 6 below.
6. Chavannes 1910, p. 302 (trans. from French, original Chinese); see chapter 4. Unless otherwise stated, all translations into English are my own.
7. Mills 1997, p. 66 (original Ketchua/Spanish).
8. Pierre Bourdieu, 'Une interprétation de la théorie de la religion selon Max Weber', *Archives européennes de Sociologie* 12 (1971): 3–21.
9. Stutfield 1918–1919, pp. 241–47; see chapter 2.
10. Jon Mathieu and Chetan Singh (eds.), Religion and Sacredness in Mountains: A Historical Perspective, Special Issue of *Mountain Research and Development* 26/4 (2006); Mathieu 2011; Xueqin/Mathieu 2014; Mathieu 2020.
11. Mountain Agenda, *An Appeal for the Mountains* (Bern 1992), p. 10.

Notes to Chapter 1

12 For a more detailed discussion of methodological aspects, see Jon Mathieu, 'Comparing Sacred Mountains: Notes on Approach and Method', in Tobias Boos and Daniela Salvucci (eds.), *Cultures of Mountain Areas. Comparative Perspectives* (Bozen, 2022), pp. 35–56,
13 Xueqin/Mathieu 2014.

Chapter 1

1 See https://translate.google.com (accessed 9 Oct. 2020).
2 Gantke 1998 (against a Catholic background); on religious studies cf. also chapter 2.
3 Carsten Colpe: 'heilig' (linguistic), in Hubert Cancik et al. (eds.), *Handbuch religionswissenschaftlicher Grundbegriffe*, vol. 3 (Stuttgart, 1993), pp. 74–80.
4 I use the English translation in *The Popes Bull, or Papal Creed Made at Trent, and Promulgated at Rome, by Pope Pius-Forth* (London 1673), pp. 22–25.
5 O'Malley 2013, pp. 118–21.
6 *Das heilige, allgültige und allgemeine Concilium von Trient* 1827, p. 74; on the number of seven cf. Josef Finkenzeller, *Die Zählung und die Zahl der Sakramente. Eine dogmengeschichtliche Untersuchung*, in: *Wahrheit und Verkündigung*, Festschrift Michael Schmaus, ed. by Leo Scheffczyk et al. (Munich 1967), vol. 2, pp. 1005–33; on the contemporary discussion, see Euan Cameron, *The European Reformation* (Oxford 2012), pp. 184–96.
7 O'Malley 2013, esp. pp. 118, 130–31, 147–48, 190, 255–56.
8 Franz X. Noppenberger, *Die eucharistische Monstranz des Barockzeitalters. Eine Studie über Geschichte, Aufbau, Dekoration, Ikonologie und Symbolik der barocken Monstranzen vernehmlich des deutschen Sprachgebietes* (Munich 1958), p. 15.
9 Rudolf Henggeler, 'Die "Grosse Monstranz" von Einsiedeln', *Zeitschrift für schweizerische Archäologie und Kunstgeschichte* **16** (1956): 35–48.
10 *Das heilige, allgültige und allgemeine Concilium von Trient* 1827, p. 312 (trans. from German, original Latin); O'Malley 2013, pp. 243–44.
11 Peter Burke, 'How to Be a Counter-Reformation Saint', in Kaspar von Greyerz (ed.), *Religion and Society in Early Modern Europe, 1500–1800* (London 1984), pp. 45–55, quote p. 50.
12 Simon Ditchfield, 'How not to Be a Counter-Reformation Saint: The Attempted Canonization of Pope Gregory X, 1622–45', *Papers of the British School at Rome* **60** (1992): 379–422.
13 Brown 1978, pp. 97–101 and Peter Brown, *The Cult of the Saints. Its Rise and Function in Latin Christianity* (Chicago 1981), pp. 121–25; in the literature, the anthropocentric character of older Christianity was often discussed in the period of critique from the 1960s onwards, cf. Ch. 11.
14 Cf. Ch. 6.

Notes to Chapter 1

15 Huber 1999, p. 60.
16 Huber 1999, p. 65 (original Tibetan), cf. also pp. 239–40, 267.
17 Huber 1999, pp. 22–25, 28–29, 72.
18 Ibid.
19 Huber 1999, 128–74.
20 Huber 1999, 119, 197–200.
21 Huber 1999b, pp. 78–79; references to this approach are also given in his unpublished dissertation, an explicit *work in progress*: Toni Huber, *What Is a Mountain? An Ethnohistory of Representation and Ritual at Pure Crystal Mountain in Tibet*, University of Canterbury 1993, at www.core.ac.uk (accessed 31 Jan. 2021).
22 Huber 1999, pp. 13–14, 22–23 and Huber 1999b, pp. 77, 79; on the complexity of Tibetan classification, see, for example, also Anne-Marie Blondeau and Ernst Steinkellner (eds.), *Reflections of the Mountain. Essays on the History and Social Meaning of the Mountain Cult in Tibet and the Himalaya* (Vienna 1996), pp. viii–ix.
23 Messner/Märtin 2013; the book is partly based on the German TV-series *Wohnungen der Götter* (Abodes of the Gods), which is not mentioned, however; the texts by the two authors are not attributed, but can generally be distinguished in terms of style and content; a second edition from 2020 under the title *Tanzplatz der Götter* (Dancing Places of the Gods) contains two short texts on the late Märtin and is otherwise unchanged.
24 Messner/Märtin 2013, pp. 237–40; with material remains alone, the exact (pre-)historical cults are difficult to infer, cf. for example the observations of Isabel Laack directed towards an 'archaeology of the future': '*Sacred Sites* in Glastonbury (England): Invention, Experience and Recording of Old and New Rituals', in Matthias Egeler (ed.), *Germanische Kultorte. Vergleiche, historische und rezeptionsgeschichtliche Zugänge* (Munich 2016), pp. 98–102.
25 Messner/Märtin 2013, p. 33.
26 Messner/Märtin 2013, p. 13, 252–55; cf. also below, Ch. 6.
27 Messner/Märtin 2013, pp. 52, 60, 214.
28 Messner/Märtin 2013, pp. 163–80; the final question is posed by the co-author Märtin.
29 Gantke 1998, p. 371.
30 *Meyers Konversations-Lexikon. Eine Encyklopädie des allgemeinen Wissens*, 4th edition, vol.12 (Leipzig 1888), p. 14.
31 Isabel Laack, 'The *New Animism* and Its Challenges to the Study of Religion', *Method and Theory in the Study of Religion* **32** (2020): 115–47.
32 Messner/Märtin 2013, pp. 20, 29–33.
33 See https://whc.unesco.org/en/list/954 (accessed 30 Oct. 2020).
34 Brown 1978, pp. 82, 89.

Notes to Chapter 2

35 Serge Brunet et al. (eds.), *Montagne sacrées d'Europe* (Paris 2005), pp. 215–62 (Part III. Déserts et ermites).
36 Émilie-Anne Pépy, *Le Territoire de la Grande Chartreuse, XVIe–XVIIe siècle. Montagne sacrée, montagne profane* (Grenoble 2011), pp. 357–68, 412 (trans. from French); cf. idem: '"Désert terrible" ou reflet de l'Eden. Représentations des montagnes, l'exemple de la Grande Chartreuse', *Geschichte der Alpen* 12 (2007): 261–72; Spanish examples in Trevor Johnson, 'Gardening for God: Carmelite Deserts and the Sacralisation of Natural Space in Counter-Reformation Spain', in Coster/Spicer 2005, pp. 193–210.
37 Martin Collcutt, *Five Mountains. The Rinzai Zen Monastic Institution in Medieval Japan* (Cambridge MA 1981); Heinrich Dumoulin, *Zen Buddhismus*, vol. II: Japan (Tübingen 2019) (2nd rev. edition), pp. 135–64; cf. Bingenheimer 2017, p. 21.
38 See the introductory remarks by Huber 1999, p. 21.
39 From different perspectives, e.g. Peter Brown, *The Rise of Western Christendom. Triumph and Diversity, AD 200–1000* (Cambridge MA 1996), pp. 20–21, 96–97, 108–09; Ramsay MacMullen, *Christianity and Paganism in the Fourth to Eighth Centuries* (New Haven 1997), pp. 64–74, 155–56, 158.
40 Of course, this does not exclude phenomena of change; however, I do not find convincing the theories that postpone the 'separation of nature and culture' to modern times, cf. chapter 11 below.
41 Miller 2011, pp. 104–33.
42 Hans-Christian Harten and Elke Harten, *Die Versöhnung mit der Natur. Gärten, Freiheitsbäume, republikanische Wälder, heilige Berge und Tugendparks in der Französischen Revolution* (Hamburg 1989), pp. 127–40; Miller 2011, pp. 133–38; the hymn in *La Chanson française du XVe au XXe siècle* (Paris 1910), p. 184.
43 Platon Blanchard, *Catéchisme de la Nature ou Religion et Morale naturelles* (Paris, Year II of the Republic, 1793/1794).
44 Mona Ozouf, *Festivals and the French Revolution* (Cambridge, MA 1988), pp. 262–82; Monique Mosser, 'Le temple et la montagne. Généalogie d'un décor de fête révolutionaire', *Revue de l'art* 83 (1989) : 21–35.
45 *Procès-verbaux du Comité d'instruction publique de la Convention nationale*, ed. by James Guillaume, vol. 5 (Paris 1904), pp. 508–09 (trans. from French).

Chapter 2

1 Ester Boserup 'Development Theory: An Analytical Framework and Selected Applications', *Population and Development Review* 22/3 (1996): 505–15; Thomas 1983, pp. 166–70; Mathieu 2011, pp. 12–13.
2 Angus Maddison, *The World Economy. A Millennial Perspective* (Paris 2001), pp. 232, 238; Rein Taagepera, 'Expansion and Contraction Patterns of

Notes to Chapter 2

Large Polities: Context for Russia', *International Studies Quarterly* **41** (1997): 475–504.

3   Landt 1994 (with separately paginated appendix: translations of the selected texts), pp. 79–95, appendix pp. 42–54 (trans. from German, original Chinese).

4   Landt 1994, pp. 142–43; Arthur W. Hummel (ed.), *Eminent Chinese of the Ch'ing Period (1644–1912)* (Taipei 1970), vol. 2, pp. 606–07; for the importance of phonology in seventeenth and eighteenth-century Neo-Confucianism, see Q. Edward Wang, 'Beyond East and West: Antiquarianism, Evidential Learning and Global Trends in Historical Study', *Journal of World History* **19**/4 (2008): 489–519; of general interest for early modern scholarly visits to sacred mountains is Dott 2004, pp. 194–224.

5   Landt 1994, p. 84.

6   Chavannes 1910, pp. 415–19 (trans. from French, original Chinese; in Chavannes the title is romanised as *Tchong-t'ien tch'ong cheng-ti*; I thank Brian R. Dott for the pinyin romanisation and translation).

7   References to literature in Robson 2009, esp. p. 335; new summaries from different points of view: Shangyi Zhou and Weilin Xu, 'Interpreting the Inheritance Mechanism of the Wu Yue Sacred Mountains in China Using Structuralist and Semiotic Approaches', *Sustainability* **10** (2018); Angelika C. Messner, 'Approaching the Sacred in Chinese Past Contexts', in Ute Luig (ed.), *Approaching the Sacred. Pilgrimage in Historical and Intercultural Perspective* (Berlin 2018), pp. 37–58; for the foreign policy dimension, see Wang Gungwu, 'Early Ming Relations with Southeast Asia: Background Essay', in John King Fairbanks (ed.), *The Chinese World Order. Traditional China's Foreign Relations* (Cambridge MA 1970), pp. 55–60, 297.

8   Robson 2009, pp. 25–26, 334–35.

9   *Power of Place* is the main title of the extensive monograph by Robson 2009; on the granting of titles and the character of office, for example, pp. 34, 41–43, 157; more generally on state rituals, Joseph P. McDermott (ed.), *State and Court Rituals in China* (Cambridge 1998).

10 E.g. Xueqin/Mathieu 2014, pp. 37–38.

11 Landt 1994, p. 85, appendix p. 44; Chavannes 1910, pp. 415–19.

12 Kai Sheng, 'On the Veneration of Four Sacred Buddhist Mountains in China', *The Eastern Buddhist* **44**/2 (2013):121–43, here pp. 126, 132.

13 Landt 1994, p. 86, appendix pp. 44, 49.

14 Qianjin Wang, 'Geoscience', in Yongxian Lu (ed.), *A History of Chinese Science and Technology* (Berlin 2015), pp. 121–202, here pp. 164–65; Laura Hostetler, 'Early Modern Mapping at the Qing Court: Survey Maps from the Kangxi, Yongzheng, and Qianlong Reign Periods', in Yongtao Du and Jeff Kyong-McClain (eds.), *Chinese History in Geographical Perspective* (Lanham, MD 2013), pp. 15–33.

Notes to Chapter 2

15 Boscani Leoni 2019, the questionnaire on pp. 33–49; the volume also contains references to the rich research literature on Scheuchzer.
16 Boscani Leoni 2019, pp. 6, 99.
17 Johann Jakob Scheuchzer, *Kupfer-Bibel, in welcher die Physica Sacra oder Geheiligte Natur-Wissenschaft derer in Heil[igen] Schrift vorkommenden Natürlichen Sachen deutlich erklärt* [wird], vol. 1 (Augsburg 1731), pp. 254–59; generally on this cultural movement: Ann Blair and Kaspar von Greyerz (eds.), *Physicotheology. Religion and Science in Europe, 1650–1750* (Baltimore 2020).
18 Cf. e.g. Sulzer 1746, 2nd part, p. 98; Boscani Leoni 2019, pp. 135–136.
19 Sulzer 1746, part 1, p. 10.
20 Sulzer 1746, part 2, pp. 316–18 and Appendix: Untersuchung von dem Ursprung der Berge, und anderer damit verknüpften Dinge, pp. 3–44; Johann Georg Sulzer, *Beschreibung einiger Merkwürdigkeiten welche er in einer Ao. 1742 gemachten Berg-Reise durch einige Oerter der Schweitz beobachtet hat* (Zurich 1747); on the French geodesy, see Walter Kertz, *Geschichte der Geophysik* (Hildesheim 1999), pp. 76–78.
21 Johann Georg Sulzer, *Versuch einiger moralischen Betrachtungen über die Werke der Natur* (Zurich 1745), pp. v–vi, 61–62.
22 Hubert Steinke, 'Sulzer, Johann Georg', in Historisches Lexikon der Schweiz, version of 17 Aug. 2012, at https://hls-dhs-dss.ch/de/articles/012337/2012-08-17/ (accessed 26 Nov. 2020).
23 Trepp 2009, pp. 330–32; for early modern changes of the 'book of nature' see e. g. James J. Bono, *The Word of God and the Languages of Man. Interpreting Nature in Early Modern Science and Medicine* (Madison 1995).
24 Johann Christoph Wolf, *Orotheologie, oder erbauliche Betrachtung über die Berge, als wichtige Zeugen der Allmacht, Weisheit, Vorsehung und Güte Gottes, und Leiter der Menschen zur schuldigen Verehrung und Anbetung, Lob und Dank, Gehorsam, Liebe und Vertrauen gegen denselben* (Hof 1756), p. 66; little is known about the author (1730–1785).
25 Trepp 2009, p. 336; Zedler, vol. 3, 1733, columns 1244–45.
26 Very broad, using the British example: Thomas 1983, for the mountains pp. 259–61.
27 Jon Mathieu and Simona Boscani Leoni (eds.) *Die Alpen! Zur europäischen Wahrnehmungsgeschichte seit der Renaissance* (Bern 2005), pp. 53–72; Mathieu 2015, pp. 138–40; Martin Korenjak, 'Why Mountains Matter. Early Modern Roots of a Modern Notion', *Renaissance Quarterly* 70 (2017): 179–219; Dawn L. Hollis: 'Mountain Gloom and Mountain Glory: The Genealogy of an Idea', *Interdisciplinary Studies in Literature and Environment* 26/4 (2019): 1038–61.
28 Alexander von Humboldt, *Researches concerning the Institutions and Monuments of the Ancient Inhabitants of America with Descriptions and Views of Some of the Most Striking Scenes* (London 1814), plate xxv (the French original was published in folio format in Paris in 1810–1813); cf. on this, Caroline

Notes to Chapter 2

Schaumann, *Peak Pursuits. The Emergence of Mountaineering in the Nineteenth Century* (New Haven 2020), pp. 63–66; on the long-term conjuncture of the concept of sublimity with literature: Pascal Gutknecht and Jon Mathieu '"Erhabene Berge". Eine korpuslinguistische Studie zu den Periodika des Schweizer Alpenclubs 1864 bis 2014', *Geschichte der Alpen* 25 (2020): 215–33.

29 Stutfield 1918–1919, pp. 241–47.
30 F.T. Wethered, 'Correspondance', *Alpine Journal* 219 (1919): 303–04.
31 Scharfe 2007, pp. 128–35; an actual prayer in Nikolai Michailowitsch Karamsin, *Briefe eines russischen Reisenden* (Berlin 1977 (first 1799–1801)), p. 269; I thank Clà Riatsch for the reference.
32 In the early modern period, the mountain of the gods had only come to prominence because of its legendary height (in reality less than 3,000 metres), its pagan sanctity or for other reasons: see, for example, Jon Mathieu: 'Der Berg als König. Aspekte der Naturwahrnehmung um 1600', *Berner Zeitschrift für Geschichte* 79/1 (2017): 3–35, here pp. 14–15; Zedler, vol. 25, 1741, columns 1383–84.
33 Constantin Klein and Thomas Schmidt-Lux, 'Ist Fußball Religion? Theoretische Perspektiven und Forschungsbefunde', in Engelbert Thaler (ed.), *Fußball. Fremdsprachen. Forschung* (Aachen 2006), pp. 18–35; Hugh McLeod, Nils Martinius Justvik and Rob Hess, 'Sport and Christianity: Historical Perspectives – An Introduction', *The International Journal of the History of Sport* 35/1 (2018): 1–8.
34 Hugh E.M. Stutfield, *The Roman Mischief-Maker. Her Teaching and Practice* (London 1919); he subsequently published two more books on religious topics.
35 Maurice Isserman and Stewart Weaver, *Fallen Giants. A History of Himalayan Mountaineering from the Age of Empire to the Age of Extremes* (New Haven 2008), pp. 108–26; Peter H. Hansen, 'The Dancing Lamas of Everest: Cinema, Orientalism, and Anglo-Tibetan Relations in the 1920s', *The American Historical Review* 101/3 (1996): 712–47, citations p. 724 and 743 (original Tibetan).
36 See, for example, Angelika C. Messner, 'Sacred Mountains and Sacred People in the Chinese Context', in Id. and Konrad Hirschler (eds.), *Heilige Orte in Asien und Afrika. Räume göttlicher Macht und menschlicher Verehrung* (Schenefeld 2006), pp. 177–98, here p. 187.
37 Mathieu 2011, pp. 27–30; there also the note that the criteria for measuring altitude have diversified in recent times; measured from the centre of the earth, Chimborazo is a good 2 kilometres higher than Mount Everest due to its location on the equator.
38 *Neue Deutsche Biographie*, vol. 1, Berlin 1953, p. 287.
39 Ferdinand von Andrian, *Der Höhencultus asiatischer und europäischer Völker. Eine ethnologische Studie* (Vienna 1891), pp. ix–xxxiv, citation p. ix; the Sino-

babylon thesis was advocated above all by the Sinologist Terrien de Lacouperie (1844–1894).
40   *Neue Deutsche Biographie*, vol. 19 (Berlin 1999), pp. 709–11.
41   Rudolf Otto, *The Idea of the Holy. An Inquiry into the Non-Rational Factor of the Divine and its Relation to the Rational* (Oxford 1924 (first German edition 1917)); on Otto as well as on Eliade there is an extensive literature to which I do not refer; here it is about the change of perspective with regard to the perception of nature; on the much-discussed relationship between theology and religious studies, for example, Karénina Kollmar-Paulenz, 'Für eine Klärung der Standorte. Zum Verhältnis von Religionswissenschaft und Theologie', *Reformatio. Zeitschrift für Kultur, Politik, Religion* 54/3 (2005): 175–81.
42   Mircea Eliade, *The Sacred and the Profane. The Nature of Religion* (New York 1957); more detailed on mountains along this line: Diana L. Eck, 'Mountains', in Mircea Eliade (ed.), *The Encyclopedia of Religion*, vol. 10 (New York 1987), pp. 130–34.
43   Eliade's involvement in right-wing extremism, especially in the 1930s, was also discussed: Daniel Dubuisson, *Impostures et pseudo-science. L'œuvre de Mircea Eliade* (Villeneuve d'Ascq 2005).
44   Ernst M. Conradie, 'An Ecological Critique of Christianity and a Christian Critique of Ecological Destruction', in Jenkins 2017, pp. 70–78; see also below chapter 11.
45   Bernbaum 1997, p. xi; in 2022 the book was re-issued with reduced illustrations and updated content. From the further literature, the following examples may be mentioned here: Samivel [Paul Gayet-Tancrède], *Hommes, cimes et dieux. Les grandes mythologies de l'altitude et la légende dorée des montagnes à travers le monde* (Paris 1973) (alpinist with a cultural interest); Karl Gratzl (ed.), *Die heiligsten Berge der Welt* (Graz 1990)(nine essays on individual mountains, introduced by a cardinal, ed. by a publishing staff member); Amilcare Barbero and Stefano Piano (eds.), *Religioni e Sacri Monti* (Ponzano Monferrato 2006) (proceedings of a large-scale interdisciplinary congress in Piedmont); Julien Ries (ed.), *Montagnes sacrées* (Paris 2010) (a good dozen essays, ed. and introduced by an archbishop).
46   Bernbaum 2006, pp. 304–09 and Bernbaum 2022, pp. 31–32, 343–50; personal communication 16 Dec. 2020.

Chapter 3

1   Toni Huber and Tsepak Rigzin, 'A Tibetan Guide for Pilgrimage to Ti-se (Mount Kailas) and mTsho Ma-pham (Lake Manasarovar)', in Toni Huber (ed.), *Sacred Spaces and Powerful Places in Tibetan Culture. A Collection of Essays* (Dharamsala 1999), pp. 125–53, here pp. 128–29 (original Tibetan); for the sake of simplification, I have listed the multi-named deities Mahadeva and

Notes to Chapter 3

Uma of the text under the more familiar names Shiva and Parvati; 'Kailash' is always rendered in this form here, even if some sources use 'Kailas' or other spellings.

2 Osterhammel 2011, p. 1250 for the figure mentioned; McKay 2015 for much information on the political context.
3 McKay 1999, pp. 305–21, here p. 308 (the author of the book was Henry Savage Landor).
4 Charles A. Sherring, *Western Tibet and the British Borderlands. The Sacred Country of Hindus and Buddhists with an Account of the Government, Religion and Customs of its Peoples* (London 1906), pp. 1–2; cf. McKay 1999, pp. 309–12 and McKay 2015, pp. 387–98.
5 Sven Hedin, *Trans-Himalaya. Discoveries and Adventures in Tibet*, vol. 2 (London 1909), p. 190.
6 McKay 2015, pp. 395–404.
7 Tichy 1937, pp. 135–55; Arnold Heim and August Gansser, *Thron der Götter. Erlebnisse der ersten Schweizerischen Himalaya-Expedition* (Zurich 1938), pp. 113–23.
8 Govinda 1966; McKay 2015, pp. 412–22.
9 Jules Blache, *L'Homme et la Montagne* (Paris 1934), pp. 99–100; Roderick Peattie, *Mountain Geography. A Critique and Field Study* (Cambridge, MA 1936), p. 4; Bernbaum 1997 (first 1990), pp. 8–15; Gratzl 1990, pp. 9–10, 81.
10 Mathieu 2011, pp. 135–36; the first connection with Everest that I know of is mentioned by McKay 2015, p. 418.
11 McKay 2015, pp. 1–21; on the controversial question of delimitability, see also Karénina Kollmar-Paulenz, 'Außereuropäische Religionsbegriffe', in Michael Stausberg (ed.), *Religionswissenschaft* (Berlin 2012), pp. 81–94.
12 McKay 2015, p. 94.
13 McKay 2015, pp. 275, 316, 322, 330–32, 364–65; Alex McKay (ed.), *The History of Tibet*, vol. 2 (London 2003), p. 787.
14 Huber 1999, pp. 23, 56, 112; mountain circumambulation also existed and still exists in Mongolia, northern parts of Nepal and perhaps in some other surrounding regions.
15 Huber 1999, pp. 17, 250 (n. 27).
16 Detailed in McKay 2015, chs 1–10.
17 Tichy 1937, p. 150; very informative for the Buddhist perception of mountain climbing is Sherry B. Ortner, *Life and Death on Mount Everest: Sherpas and Himalayan Mountaineering* (Princeton 1999).
18 Swami Pranavananda, *Kailas – Manasarovar* (Calcutta 1949), pp. 82–83.
19 Govinda 1966; Hellmuth Hecker, *Lebensbilder deutscher Buddhisten. Ein bio-bibliographisches Handbuch*, vol. 1: Die Gründer (Konstanz 1996), pp. 84–115.
20 Govinda 1966, pp. 197–200.

Notes to Chapter 4

21 Govinda 1966, pp. 147–49, 204–09, 216, 267–76.
22 Frankfurter Rundschau, 28 Aug. 2003; documentation of the Tibet Initiative Germany at www.tibet-initiative.de (accessed 28 Dec. 2008); later the road construction plan was dropped by the Chinese authorities.
23 John Snelling, *The Sacred Mountain. Travellers and Pilgrims at Mount Kailas in Western Tibet and the Great Universal Symbol of the Sacred Mountain* (Delhi 2006), pp. 313–80; Katrin Burri, *Umweltschutz in der Kailashregion. Präfektur Ngari, West Tibet. Eine Situationsanalyse* (s.l. , Zurich/Kriens 2005), p. 7; in religiously emphasised years, the flow of pilgrims could greatly exceed the number mentioned.
24 Anna Urbanska-Szymoszyna, 'Transforming Tibetan Icon. Chinese Impact and Global Implications on the Picture of Mt. Kailas', *The Tibet Journal* 36/4 (2011): 35.

Chapter 4

1 A multi-faceted study of the older period is offered by Brian R. Dott, *Identity Reflections. Pilgrimages to Mount Tai in Later Imperial China* (Cambridge, MA 2004); a classic is Edouard Chavannes, *Le T'ai Chan. Essai de monographie d'un culte chinois* (Paris 1910). As can be seen from these book titles, the romanised spelling of Tai Shan varies; the Chinese spelling is: 泰山.
2 World Heritage Nomination – IUCN Summary, no. 437, May 1987, in UNESCO Resources Archive, at https://whc.unesco.org/en/documents/153475 (accessed 1 Feb. 2021).
3 Harrist 2008, p. 289 (original Chinese).
4 Harrist 2008, pp. 254–58 (original Chinese); for *Tai* or *Dai* see also Dott 2004, p. 31.
5 Harrist 2008, pp. 18, 24, 26, 284–87, 302 (n. 26).
6 Chavannes 1910, pp. 6–7 (trans. from French, original Chinese).
7 Chavannes 1910, pp. 288–93.
8 Dott 2004, pp. 66, 73; Chavannes 1910, p. 28 (trans. from French, original Chinese).
9 Dott 2004, pp. 56, 203, 221–22.
10 Daniel L. Overmyer, 'Religion in China Today – Introduction', *The China Quarterly* (Special Issue) 174 (2003): 308; André Laliberté and Stefania Travagnin (eds.), *Concepts and Methods for the Study of Chinese Religions*, vol. 1 (Berlin 2019), p. 4.
11 Dott 2004, pp. 88, 110–15, 293–94.
12 Dott 2004, pp. 121–30, 265–67; Chavannes 1910, pp. 70–72; Pei-yi Wu, 'An Ambivalent Pilgrim to T'ai Shan in the Seventeenth Century', in Susan Naquin and Chün-fang Yü (eds.), *Pilgrims and Sacred Sites in China* (Berkeley 1992), pp. 65–88, here p. 65.

Notes to Chapter 5

13 Mark Elvin, *The Retreat of the Elephants. An Environmental History of China* (New Haven 2004), pp. 407–08; Dott 2004, pp. 88–100.
14 Pomeranz 1997, pp. 182–204.
15 Pomeranz 1997, pp. 182–83.
16 Kenneth Pomeranz, 'Orthopraxy, Orthodoxy, and the Goddess(es) of Taishan', *Modern China* **33**/1 (2017): 22–46, here 30–31; on the ritual location of the male god: Dott 2004, pp. 183–84.
17 Kouamé/Goossaert 2006, p. 216.
18 Kouamé/Goossaert 2006, pp. 204–05, 215–18.
19 Daniel L. Overmyer, *Local Religion in North China in the Twentieth Century. The Structure and Organisation of Community Rituals and Beliefs* (Leiden 2009), pp. 50–51; the historiography of the Cultural Revolution is very controversial: see Barbara Barnouin and Yu Changgen, *Ten Years of Turbulence. The Chinese Cultural Revolution* (London 1993); Mobo Gao, *The Battle for China's Past: Mao and the Cultural Revolution* (London 2008).
20 Dott 2004, p. 43; Dott 2010, p. 323; Harrist 2008, pp. 287–89.
21 Dott 2004, pp. 232–34, 294; Dott 2010; Brian R. Dott, 'Taishan yu minzuzhuyi: yizuo shengdi xiangzheng guojia' (Mount Tai and Nationalism: A Sacred Site Symbolizes the Nation), *Minzu yanjiu* (Folklore Studies) (2018, no. 2): 74–79; some experts warn against underestimating religious continuities in modern China: see Vincent Goossaert, 'For a History of Religious Ideas in Modern and contemporary China', in André Laliberté and Stefania Travagnin (eds.), *Concepts and Methods for the Study of Chinese Religions*, vol. 1 (Berlin 2019), pp. 231–49, here p. 234.
22 World Heritage Nomination – IUCN Summary 1987, no. 437, May 1987, in UNESCO Resources Archive, at https://whc.unesco.org/en/documents/153475 (accessed 1 Feb. 2021).
23 Cf. https://whc.unesco.org/en/tentativelists/state=cn (accessed 5 Feb. 2021).
24 Nomination of Kailash Sacred Landscape as World Heritage Site, 27 Jan. 2016, at https://wii.gov.in/images//images/documents/unesco_c2c_nwhs_nom_kailash_2016.pdf (accessed 5 Feb. 2021) and personal communication from Edwin Bernbaum, who led the preliminary negotiations (16 Dec. 2020).

Chapter 5

1 *20 Minuten*, 23 Dec. 2011 (trans. from German); in the following chapter I adapt several passages from Mathieu 2020.
2 *Pamela Kyle Crossley: The Manchus* (Cambridge, MA 1997) (for the Changbaishan terms pp. 206–07).
3 Elliott 2000, p. 612 (original Chinese).
4 Elliott 2000, p. 613; Stephen H. Whiteman, *Where Dragon Veins Meet. The Kangxi Emperor and His Estate at Rehe* (Washington 2020), p. 67.

Notes to Chapter 5

5   Pamela Kyle Crossley, 'An Introduction to the Qing Foundation Myth', *Late Imperial China* **6**/2 (1985): 13–24; Lin Sun, 'Writing an Empire: An Analysis of the Manchu Origin Myth and the Dynamics of Manchu Identity', *Journal of Chinese History* **1** (2017): 93–109.
6   Dott 2004, pp. 33 and 161–62 (original Chinese).
7   Elliott 2000, p. 614.
8   Seonmin Kim, *Ginseng and Borderland. Territorial Boundaries and Political Relations between Qing China and Choson Korea 1636–1912* (Oakland, CA 2017), pp. 58–59, 71–72 (original Korean).
9   Grayson 2015.
10 Grayson 2015; Yuanchong Wang, 'Provincializing Korea: The Construction of the Chinese Empire in the Borderland and the Rise of the Modern Chinese State', *T'oung Pao* **105** (2019): 128–82, here pp. 136–37, 141.
11 Marion Egger, 'View of the Country, Visions of Self. Choson Dynasty Travel Records on Chiri-san and Paektu-san', *Asiatische Studien* **52** (1998): 1069–102.
12 Chizuko T. Allen, 'Northeast Asia Centered Around Korea: Ch'oe Namson's View of History', *The Journal of Asian Studies* **49**/4 (1990): 787–806; Hyung Il Pay, *Constructing 'Korean' Origins. A Critical Review of Archeology, Historiography, and Racial Myth in Korean State-Formation Theories* (Cambridge, MA 2000); Andre Schmid, *Korea Between Empires, 1985–1919* (New York 2002).
13 Timothy S. Lee, 'What Should Christians Do about a Shaman-Progenitor? Evangelicals and Ethnic Nationalism in South Korea', *Church History* **78**/1 (2009): 66–98.
14 Michael J. Seth, *A Concise History of Modern Korea. From Late Nineteenth Century to the Present* (London 2006), p. 237.
15 Virginie Grzelczyk, 'In the Name of the Father, Son, and Grandson: Succession Patterns and the Kim Dynasty', *The Journal of Northeast Asian History* **9**/2 (2012): 33–68.
16 Socialist Constitution of the Democratic People's Republic of Korea, Pyongyang 1998, Article 163.
17 *Kim il Sung 1993–2007*, vol. 1, pp. 261–264; original Korean, two of these volumes published posthumously; the book appears to be popular and widely used in North Korea.
18 Kim il Sung 1993–2007, vol. 8. p. 387.
19 Suh 1988.
20 Lim 2015.
21 Lim 2015, p. 55; a detailed reconstruction in Suh 1988.
22 Lim 2015, p. 72; the figures refer to the period since 1956, but it can be assumed that visits have risen sharply since the campaigns of the 1980s; since in-country travel is also subject to state control, the figure may not be based on estimates alone.

Notes to Chapter 6

23   Alpines Museum der Schweiz (ed.), *Let's Talk About Mountains* (Begleitpublikation zur Nordkorea-Ausstellung) (Bern 2020), p. 106; the publication documents the significance of Paektusan in current everyday culture.
24   On the concept of family resemblance in religious studies, see Ch. 11.
25   Approaches to the systematisation of sacred mountains existed in several regions, in territorial terms especially among Indian nations in the south-west of the USA (see Bernbaum 1997, pp. 157–61); to what extent one should compare this with the elaborate Chinese mountain culture would be debatable.
26   Andrea Castiglioni, Fabio Rambelli and Carina Roth (eds.), *Defining Shugendo. Critical Studies on Japanese Mountain Religion* (London 2020); the uniqueness is also emphasised by Bernbaum 1997, p. 60.
27   Cf. Osterhammel 2011, esp. pp. 1248–58.

Chapter 6

1   When Reinhold Messner describes the European mountains as the 'territory of ghosts, witches and monsters' (cf. chapter 1), he is referring to a widespread view of popular history; on the cross and crucifix in early modern popular literature, cf. *Enzyklopädie des Märchens. Handwörterbuch zur historischen und vergleichenden Erzählforschung*, begründet von Kurt Ranke, vol. 8, Berlin 1996, columns 387–398, 511–515.
2   Wendy Griffin, 'The Embodied Goddess: Feminist Witchcraft and Female Divinity', *Sociology of Religion* **56**/1 (1995): 35–48; Vincenzo Lavenia, 'The Alpine Model of Witchcraft. The Italian Context in the Early Modern Period', in Marco Bellabarba et al. (eds.), *Communities and Conflicts in the Alps from the Late Middle Ages to Early Modernity* (Bologna 2015), pp. 151–164; Mathieu 2015, pp. 113–119.
3   Andreas Bodenstein von Karlstadt, *Von abtuhung der Bylder, Und das keyn Betdler unther den Christen seyn soll* (Wittenberg 1522), pp. 8, 10 (trans. from German).
4   Peter Blickle et al. (eds.), *Macht und Ohnmacht der Bilder. Reformatorischer Bildersturm im Kontext der europäischen Geschichte* (Munich 2002); Coster/Andrew 2005; Jaroslav Pelikan, *Reformation of Church and Dogma (1300–1700)* (Chicago 1984), pp. 216–17.
5   *Das heilige, allgültige und allgemeine Concilium von Trient 1827*, pp. 313–314 (trans. from German, original Latin).
6   O'Malley 2013, pp. 260–61; Keith P. Luria, *Territories of Grace. Cultural Change in the Seventeenth-Century Diocese of Grenoble* (Berkeley 1991), pp. 67–68, 77; Zwyssig 2018, part 3; Rime 2021, pp. 135–48, 500.
7   Hippolyte Delehaye, *The Legends of the Saints. An Introduction to Hagiography* (London 1907), pp. 173–74.

Notes to Chapter 6

8   Jon Mathieu, 'The Sacralization of Mountains in Europe during the Modern Age', *Mountain Research and Development* **26**/4 (2006): 343–49, here p. 343.
9   Important for the emergence of this monastic-montane movement in the eastern Mediterranean may have been the substrate at the time of transition to Christianity; there was an ancient tradition here of prominent mountain shrines (probably different from in western regions), which were later reshaped by Christian monasticism: cf. the contributions by Herbert Niehr and Johannes Hahn in Kasper/Rollinger 2023.
10 Speake 2018, p. 49.
11 The builder was the Ecumenical Patriarch (and Freemason) Joakim III; personal communication from Steffen Züfle, Gemeinschaft der Freunde des Agion Oros Athos e. V., on 6 March 2021. It would have to be checked whether there was a now-lost predecessor building; in the extensive Athos literature, the summit story receives little attention; two descriptions from 1943 and 1994 in Rudolf Billetta (ed.), *Europa erlesen: Athos* (Klagenfurt 2000), pp. 263–71, 299–301.
12 *Wiener Zeitschrift für Kunst, Literatur, Theater und Mode*, 17 Feb. 1824, 171–73 (trans. from German).
13 See, for example ,Stéphane Gal, *Histoires verticales. Les usages politiques et culturels de la montagne (XIVe–XVIIIe siècles)* (Ceyzérieu 2018), pp. 157–58 (most used on ecclesiastical buildings); Zwyssig 2018, p. 162 (around a secondary settlement); Rime 2021, pp. 135–39 (on Alpine pastures and foothills of the Alps); crosses were also used to mark national borders and pass crossings.
14 Löwer 2019, p. 8 gives a figure of 3,000–4,000; for the context of early mountain research, see also Daniel Anker, 'Das Kreuz mit dem Kreuz. Gipfelkreuze sind weltweit verbreitet. Ein Streifzug', *Die Alpen* 04 (2012): 56–63.
15 Tyrol and Fribourg are also the regions on which special literature has been produced, especially Kunz 2012; Rime 2021.
16 Marianne Klemun, *... mit Madame Sonne konferieren. Die Großglockner-Expeditionen 1799 und 1800* (Klagenfurt 2000), pp. 148, 151, 153, 157, 163, 179, 347.
17 Martin Scharfe, 'Kruzifix mit Blitzableiter', *Österreichische Zeitschrift für Volkskunde* **53**/102 (1999): 289–336 (a pioneering essay, but constructing an artificial opposition between religion and the Enlightenment manifested in the lightning rod); see also Scharfe 2007, pp. 268–75; on the political trend, see Jon Mathieu, Eva Bauchmann and Ursula Butz, *Majestätische Berge. Die Monarchie auf dem Weg in die Alpen 1760–1910* (Baden 2018).
18 Löwer 2019, pp. 26–29.
19 Kunz 2012, pp. 63–68; Löwer 2019, pp. 59–62.
20 Löwer 2019, pp. 306–09.
21 Personal communication from Ans Puorger, Ramosch, 23 March 2021 (on Piz Arina between 1997 and 2000); two other summit crosses in the Lower

Notes to Chapter 7

Engadine are on the border with Catholic Austria and were set from there (Piz Buin, Fluchthorn/Piz Fenga); among the hundred summit crosses listed by Löwer 2019, only one cross from 2007 is in a Protestant area (pp. 271–72).

22   There is a extensive literature on the painting and Ramdohr controversy; the texts from 1809 are in Sigrid Hinz (ed.), *Caspar David Friedrich in Briefen und Bekenntnissen* (Munich 1974), pp. 131–88, quotations pp. 149–51 (trans. from German); on the arguments mentioned, see also pp. 166–67, 170, 183.

23   Eugen Guido Lammer, 'Naturfreunde und Naturschutz', in Eugen Guido Lammer 1999, pp. 120–32 (first 1928), quote p. 130 (trans. from German); he sometimes characterised 'unadulterated nature' with pantheistic religious expressions; cf. his 'Sermon on the Mount' in Eugen Guido Lammer, *Jungborn. Bergfahrten und Höhengedanken eines einsamen Pfadsuchers* (Munich 1923), pp. 161–63.

24   Eugen Guido Lammer 1999 (1928), p. 127 (trans. from German).

25   Löwer 2019, pp. 53–57, 322–25; https://frei-denken.ch/news (accessed 10 March 2010: 'Gipfelkreuze beschädigen: keine Verletzung der Religionsfreiheit'); 'Pourfendeur et défenseur de la croix face à face', *La Gruyère*, 18 March 2010.

26   Denise Sonney, *Présence sur la montagne en terre fribourgeoise* (Fribourg 2012), p. 7 (trans. from French); for the religious background in the region: Rime 2012, pp. 554–70.

27   Löwer 2019, p. 319 (trans. from German).

28   Luigi Corvi, 'Buddha o croce, la sfida in vetta', *Corriere della Sera*, 9 Set. 2005 (trans. from Italian); Marco Volken, *Badile. Kathedrale aus Granit* (Zurich 2006), p. 212; various observations on Alpine Buddhism: Bernhard Tschofen, 'Die verlängerten Alpen. Skizzen zur europäischen Tibetsehnsucht', *Schweizerisches Archiv für Volkskunde* 99 (2003): 65–82; Mathieu Petite, *Identités en chantiers dans les Alpes. Des projets qui mobilisent objets, territoires et réseaux* (Bern 2011), pp. 213–20, 315–17; Kunz 2012, pp. 201–05.

Chapter 7

1   For the following, especially Marco Cuaz, '"Preti Alpinisti". Scienza cristiana e disciplinamento sociale alle origini dell'alpinismo cattolico', in Jon Mathieu and Simona Boscani Leoni (eds.), *Die Alpen! Zur europäischen Wahrnehmungsgeschichte seit der Renaissance* (Bern 2005), pp. 279–97; Marco Cuaz, 'Alpinismo cattolico', in Aldo Audisio and Alessandro Pastore (eds.), *CAI 150. Il libro* (Torino 2013), pp. 91–109; cf. Andrea Zannini, *Tonache e piccozze. Il clero e la nascita dell'alpinismo* (Torino 2004) and, on the context, Marco Cuaz, *Le Alpi*, (Bologna 2005); Alessandro Pastore, *Alpinismo e storia d'Italia. Dall'Unità alla Resistenza* (Bologna 2003).

Notes to Chapter 7

2   Abbé [Joseph-Marie] Henry, *Brins de vie, d'histoire et de poésie. Recueil d'ouvrages* (Valpelline 1997), p. 20 (trans. from French).
3   Fabrini 1991 (first published 1945); Gabriele De Rosa, *Storia del movimento cattolico in Italia. Dalla Restaurazione all'età giolittiana* (Bari 1966), vol. 1, esp. pp. 37, 76–77, 81–86, 153, 162–63, 242–43.
4   Fabrini 1991, for the topics addressed e.g. pp. 38, 46, 75–76, 82, 91–92, 98, 149, 160, 235–36; see also Romolo Comandini, 'Il noviziato giornalistico di Giovanni Acquaderni e i temi della sua propaganda politico-religiosa nel territorio delle ex-Legazioni', *Studi Romagnoli* 30 (1968): 437–50; for an international overview of Catholic publishing, Heinz Nauer, *Fromme Industrie. Der Benziger Verlag Einsiedeln 1750–1970* (Baden 2017), pp. 217–48.
5   Fabrini 1991, pp. 169–73; on the political context, Gilles Ferragu, 'Le jubilé de l'année 1900', in Pontificio comitato di scienze storiche (ed.), *I giubilei nella storia della chiesa* (Rome 2001), pp. 632–42.
6   Fabrini 1991, p. 177; sometimes this idea is dated back to 1896 and Leo XIII is credited as the author; at the meeting of the Opera dei Congressi in Fiesole at that time, however, only the general dedication of the Jubilee Year 1900 to the Redeemer seems to have been discussed.
7   Circular letter of the Roman Committee of 8 July 1899 (trans. from Italian), quoted in Gaspari 2021, p. 13; I thank Oscar Gaspari (Rome) and Gerardo De Meo (Formia) for providing the map.
8   Fabrini 1991, p. 184; personal communication from Oscar Gaspari, 11 April 2021.
9   Gaspari 2021, p. 51.
10 Gaspari 2021, pp. 17–24; Marco Cuaz, 'Barometri, croci e bandiere. Rituali di vetta e usi pubblici della montagna nelle Alpi del Sette e Ottocento', in Pier Paolo Viazzo and Ricardo Cerri (eds.), *Da montagna a montagna. Mobilità e migrazioni interne nelle Alpi italiane (secoli XVII–XIX)* (Alagna Valsesia 2009), pp. 49–63, here pp. 61–63.
11 Ludovico Bich (ed.), *Whymper, Carrel & Company. Una croce, 400 foto, un altro Cervino* (Aosta 1997), pp. 37 and 40 (trans. from French).
12 *Tametsi futura prospicientibus*, Encylical of Pope Leo XIII on Jesus Christ the Redeemer: www.vatican.va (accessed 8 April 2021), section 10 (original Latin).
13 The *sacri monti* in parts of northern Italy were different from the potential *monti sacri*: see Jon Mathieu 'Sacri Monti (collective review)', Hsozkult, 8 July 2019.
14 Fabrini 1991, p. 75.
15 Lucia Grinberg, 'República Católica – Cristo Redentor', in Paula Knauss (ed.), *Cidade Vaidosa. Imagens urbanas do Rio de Janeiro* (Rio de Janeiro 1999), pp. 57–72, quote p. 70 (trans. from Portuguese); Emerson Giumbelli, 'Brasileiro e europeu: a construção da nacionalidade em torno do monumento ao Cristo Redentor do Corcovado', *Cadernos de Antropologia e Imagen* 24/1 (2007):

Notes to Chapter 8

35–63; Antônio Sérgio Ribeiro, 'Cristo Redentor: 80 anos de um simbolo', Agência de Notícias da Assemblea Legislativa de São Paolo 2011: https://www.al.sp.gov.br/noticia/?id=310849 (accessed 9 April 2021); in the literature I reviewed, the explicit connection to the Cristo Redentore of the Jubilee Year 1900 is missing; however, the model of the clearly related Cristo Redentor de los Andes of 1904 and the close ties to the Vatican are often mentioned; the very name of the statue speaks of a certain historical dependence.

Chapter 8

1   DeMallie 1984, pp. 48, 295 (original Lakota language).
2   The literary-style conversation became a classic *Black Elk Speaks. Being the Life Story of a Holy Man of the Oglala Sioux as Told through John G. Neihardt* (Albany 2008) (first 1932); DeMaille 1984 offers an annotated edition based on the recording transcripts.
3   US name documents from 1930 and 1980 at https://geonames.usgs.gov (accessed 6 May 2021).
4   Matthew Glass, '"Alexander's All". Symbols of Conquest and Resistance at Mount Rushmore', in David Chidester and Edward T. Linenthal (eds.), *American Sacred Space* (Bloomington 1995), pp. 152–86, quotes p. 158.
5   Larner 2002, pp. 10–12.
6   Larner 2002, pp. 106, 118.
7   Larner 2002, pp. 243–44, 263.
8   Kiara M. Vigil, 'Who Was Henry Standing Bear? Remembering Lakota Activism from the Early Twentieth Century', *Great Plains Quarterly* 37 (2017): 157–82.
9   Lawrence Downes, 'Waiting for Crazy Horse', *The New York Times*, 1 Sept. 2009.
10 Linea Sundstrom, *Storied Stone: Indian Rock Art in the Black Hills Country* (Norman 2004).
11 On regional history, Raymond J. DeMallie (ed.), 'Plains', *Handbook of North American Indians*, vol. 13 (Washington 2001); Ostler 2010; Manuel Menrath, *Mission Sitting Bull. The Cultural Conquest of the Sioux and their Varied Response* (Morgantown 2017); generally, Colin G. Calloway, *First Peoples. A Documentary Survey of American Indian History* (Boston 1999); Aram Mattioli, *Verlorene Welten. Eine Geschichte der Indianer Nordamerikas 1700–1910* (Stuttgart 2017); Heike Bungert, *Die Indianer. Geschichte der indigenen Nationen in den USA* (Munich 2020).
12 Ostler 2010, pp. 58–103.
13 DeMallie 1984, pp. 65–66.
14 The most detailed study is offered by Linea Sundstrom, 'The Sacred Black Hills. An Ethnohistorical Review', *Great Plains Quarterly* 17 (1997): 185–212;

Notes to Chapter 8

she also discusses the authors who dispute the sacredness claims; for a regional overview see Raymond J. DeMallie, 'Lakota Belief and Ritual in the Nineteenth Century', in Raymond J. DeMallie and Douglas R. Parks (eds.), *Sioux Indian Religion. Tradition and Innovation* (Norman 1987), pp. 25–43; for the variability of Indigenous beliefs, see Christian F. Feest, *Beseelte Welten. Die Religionen der Indianer Nordamerikas* (Freiburg i. Br. 1998); in the Spanish colonial empire of Central and South America, writing goes back further; there is evidence as early as the 17th century that religious addresses were occasionally addressed to the mountains, see e.g. Mills 1997 (cf. the quotation from this in the foreword above).

15   Larner 2002, p. 285; generally, Wilcomb E. Washburn, 'The Native American Renaissance, 1960 to 1995', in Bruce G. Trigger and Wilcomb E. Washburn (eds.), *The Cambridge History of the Native Peoples of the Americas*, vol. 1: North America, part 2 (Cambridge 1996), pp. 401–73.

16   Robin K. Rannow, 'Religion: The First Amendment and the American Indian Religious Freedom Act of 1978', *American Indian Law Review* **10**/1 (1982): 151–66; Anita Parlow, 'Cry, Sacred Ground: Big Mountain, U.S.A.', *American Indian Law Review* **14**/2 (1989): 301–22.

17   Ostler 2010, pp. 167–91.

18   Bernhard Gissibl, Sabine Höhler and Patrick Kupper (eds.), *Civilizing Nature. National Parks in Global Historical Perspective* (New York 2012).

19   Bron Taylor, 'Resacralizing Earth: Pagan Environmentalism and the Restoration of Turtle Island', in David Chidester and Edward T. Linenthal (eds.), *American Sacred Space* (Bloomington 1995), pp. 97–151, here pp. 100–04; Roderick Frazier Nash, *Wilderness and the American Mind* (New Haven 2001), pp. 167–68; on the linguistic bifurcation of *wilderness/desert* in the King James Bible and the Luther Bible, see. Jon Mathieu, 'Mountain Wilderness. Mit einem Begriff die Alpen verteidigen', *Geschichte der Alpen* **27** (2022): 31–45.

20   For the specifically Buddhist influence on the US West Coast, see the book by Walter Yeeling Evans-Wentz, who maintained contacts with the German-Indian Buddhist Anagarika Govinda, mentioned in Ch. 3: *Cuchama and Sacred Mountains* (Athens, OH 1981); in addition, the specialist anthropological assessment in *Journal of California and Great Basin Anthropology* **5** /2 (1983): 279–80.

21   Today, the 'founding generation' is sometimes sharply criticised for its behaviour: see Darryl Fears and Steven Mufson, 'Liberal, Progressive – and Racist? The Sierra Club Faces Its White Supremacist History', *The Washington Post*, 22 July 2020.

22   Shepard Krech III, *The Ecological Indian. Myth and History* (London 1999); Bernbaum: 2006, p. 307.

23   Larner 2002, p. 323.

24   Larner 2002, pp. 323–330.

Notes to Chapter 9

25 Larner 2002, p. 321.
26 See https://en.wikipedia.org/wiki/Black_Elk (accessed 11 May 2021).

Chapter 9

1   Krapf 1964, 2nd part, pp. 30–31 (trans. from German); the psalm according to the King James Bible; Rebmann was travelling on behalf of the British Church Missionary Society and used an English Bible.
2   From the extensive literature: Albert Wirz, Andreas Eckert and Katrin Bromber (eds.), *Alles unter Kontrolle. Disziplinierungsprozesse im kolonialen Tansania (1850–1960)* (Cologne 2003); Bernhard Gissibl, *The Nature of German Imperialism. Conservation and the Politics of Wildlife in Colonial East Africa* (New York 2016); Lars Kreye, *'Deutscher Wald' in Afrika. Koloniale Konflikte um regenerative Ressourcen, Tansania 1892–1916* (Göttingen 2021).
3   Dundas 1924, quote p. 38.
4   Dundas 1924, p. 107.
5   Dundas 1924, pp. 39, 136, 181, 192; on his working methods, see Stahl 1964, pp. 16–17.
6   Bernbaum 1997 (first edition 1990), p. 137.
7   Stahl 1964, pp. 19–20, 40–41, 393 (keyword: shrines).
8   UNESCO Resources Archive: Advisory Board Evaluation (IUCN), 403-IUCN-466.en.pdf at https://whc.unesco.org/en/documents/153391; Report of the World Heritage Eleventh Session, 7–11 Dec.1987: https://whc.unesco.org/en/decisions/3754 (accessed 23 Aug. 2021).
9   John Iliffe, *A Modern History of Tanganyika* (Cambridge 1979), pp. 26–34, 81–87, 203–39, 537–52.
10 Krapf 1964, part 1, pp. 210, 403 (trans. from German); see also Heinrich Bursik, *'Wissenschaft u. Mission soll sich auf innigste miteinander befreunden'. Geographie und Sprachwissenschaft als Instrumente der Mission – der Afrikareisende Johann Ludwig Krapf*, thesis University of Vienna 2008: http://othes.univie.ac.at/404/ (accessed 6 Aug. 2021).
11 Krapf 1964, part 2, pp. 268–269 and Johann Ludwig Krapf: 'Kurze Beschreibung der Masai- und Wakuasi-Stämme im südöstlichen Afrika', *Das Ausland. Eine Wochenschrift für Kunde des geistigen und sittlichen Lebens der Völker*, 1857, pp. 437–442, 461–466, here pp. 438, 442 (translated from German).
12 Fischer 1883–84, p. 72; on his general attitude see also Gustav A. Fischer, *Mehr Licht im dunklen Weltteil. Betrachtungen über die Kolonisation des tropi- schen Afrika unter besonderer Berücksichtigung des Sansibar-Gebiets* (Berlin 1885).
13 Thomas Alexander Barns, *Across the Great Craterland to the Congo* (London 1923), pp. 57–59; on blood and milk, e.g. Fischer 1883–84, pp. 68–69; Kaj

Notes to Chapter 10

Arhem, 'Maasai Food Symbolism. The Cultural Connotation of Milk, Meat, and Blood in Maasai Diet', *Anthropos* 84 (1989): 1–23.

14 Moritz Merker, *Die Masai. Ehnographische Monographie eines ostafrikanischen Semitenvolkes* (Berlin 1910) (quite detailed on religious beliefs around the god Ngai, but no reference to the volcano Ol Doinyo Lengai); Thomas Spear and Richard Waller (eds.), *Being Maasai. Ethnicity and Identity in East Africa* (Oxford 1993) (no references to mountains as ethno-religious references).

15 Richard Lyamuya et al., 'Human-carnivore Conflict over Livestock in the Eastern Part of the Serengeti Ecosystem, with a Particular Focus on the African Wild Dog Lycaon Pictus', *Oryx* (July 2014): www.researchgate.net (accessed 22 Aug. 2021); 'No End in Sight to Loliondo Conflict as Protagonists Dig In', *The East African*, 22 Dec. 2014: www.theeastafrican.co.ke (accessed 22 Aug. 2021).

16 Messner/Märtin 2013, pp. 46–61, here p. 59.

17 A study of Mount Kenya, which is sometimes mentioned in this context, is likely to come to similar conclusions; the classic description by Jomo Kenyatta (*Facing Mount Kenya*, London 1938) only refers to the mountain dwelling of the deity and to regulations on ritual direction on some occasions. Ute Luig and Achim von Oppen also provide clues for a general assessment: 'Einleitung: Zur Vergesellschaftung von Natur in Afrika', in ibidem (eds.), *Naturaneignung in Afrika als sozialer und symbolischer Prozess* (Berlin 1995), pp. 5–28; Molefi Kete Asante and Ama Mazama (eds.), *Encyclopedia of African Religion*, 2 vols (Thousand Oaks 2009).

Chapter 10

1 'Ayers Rock Returns', *Tribune* (Sydney), 30 Oct. 1985; 'Ayers Rock "Mystic to All Australians"', *The Canberra Times*, 21 May 1985; on the media context, see Whittacker 1994. The title to the 'Rock' went to the Indigenous group of the Anangu, who, however, had to lease it to the Australian government or the Uluru-Kata Tjuta National Park for 99 years immediately after the handover.

2 Spencer 1896, vol. 1, pp. 85–90.

3 Spencer 1896, p. 90; later the name of the witness was written down as Lungkatitukukana (without the r) and combined with another personal name (Lungkata Tjukurrpa); see Layton 1986, p. 55; after visiting a neighbouring inselberg, the expedition met another Indigenous group.

4 Baldwin Spencer and Francis James Gillen, *The Natives Tribes of Central Australia* (London 1899). For their extensive work, see the scholarly website: http://spencerandgillen.net/resources (accessed 1 Nov. 2022).

5 In 1913, Bronislaw Malinowski said that, since Spencer and Gillen's publications, half of anthropological works referred to them and nine-tenths were influenced by them; see Philip Batty and Jason Gibson: 'Reconstructing the

Notes to Chapter 10

    Spencer and Gillen Collection online. Museums, Indigenous Perspectives and the Production of Cultural Knowledge in the Digital Age', in Holger Meyer et al. (eds.), *Corpora ethnographica online. Strategien der Digitalisierung kultureller Archive und ihrer Präsentation im Internet* (Münster 2014), pp. 29–48.

6   Durkheim 1912.

7   Gaston Richard, 'L'athéisme dogmatique en sociologie religieuse', *Revue d'histoire et de philosophie religieuse* **3** (1923): 125–37 (the expression *métaphysique aventureuse* p. 126) and 229–261; on the background to the dispute, see William S.F. Pickering and Michel Bozon, 'Gaston Richard: collaborateur et adversaire', *Revue française de sociologie* (1979): 163–82.

8   Durkheim 1912, pp. 49–58.

9   An early description of the Dreamtime is found in Adolph Peter Elkin, *The Australian Aboriginals. How to Understand Them* (Sydney 1930), pp. 177–79; I borrow here from the practice-oriented text by Philip Batty, *A Secret History: The Collection and Repatriation of Aboriginal Sacred Objects*: www.academia.edu (accessed 3 Sept. 2021).

10   Charles P. Mountford, *Brown Men and Red Sand. Journeys in Wild Australia* (London 1950), p. 79 (the scene refers to a 1940 visit); for later more detailed versions: William E. Harney, 'Ritual and Behaviour at Ayers Rock', *Oceania* 30–31 (1960): 63–75; Charles P. Mountford, *Ayers Rock. Its People, Their Beliefs and Their Art* (Sydney 1965), pp. 31–154; Layton 1986, pp. 3–16, 40–43, 119–25.

11   Jillian Barnes, 'Tourism and Place-Making at Uluru (Ayers Rock). From Wasteland to Spiritual Birthing Site, 1929–1958', *International Journal of Humanities* **3**/9 (2005/2006): 77–104; Barnes 2011.

12   Frank Clune, 'Ayer's Rock (Said to Be the Largest Rock of the World),' *Walkabout. Australia's Geographic Magazine*, Oct.1941, 11–15.

13   John Béchervaise, 'Schoolboy Exploration in Australia', *Australian Geographical Walkabout Magazine*, Dec. 1950, 32–35; cf. Barnes 2011, pp. 157, 165–66, 172.

14   Barnes 2011, p. 165.

15   William E. Harney, 'The Dome of Uluru', *Australian Geographical Walkabout Magazine*, Oct.1957, 32–35.

16   Bill (William E.) Harney, *To Ayers Rock and Beyond* (Bayswater 1988) (first 1963), for the tourist figure, p. 120; see also Layton 1986, pp. 40, 44, 76, 117–20; *The Encyclopedia of Aboriginal Australia*, ed. by David Horton (Canberra 1994), vol. 1, p. 451.

17   Whittacker 1994, pp. 316–17, 328.

18   From an illuminating perspective, Philip Batty, 'Private Politics, Public Strategies: White Advisers and Their Aboriginal Subjects', *Oceania* **75**/3 (2005): 202–21.

19   Layton 1986, pp. 93–104.

Notes to Chapter 11

20 Layton 1986, pp. 105–18; Aboriginal Areas Protection Authority: https://www.aapant.org.au/ (accessed 18 Sept. 2021).
21 Ronald M. Berndt, *Australian Aboriginal Religion* (Leiden 1975), p. vi; Charles P. Mountford, *Ayers Rock. Its People, Their Beliefs and Their Art*, 2nd edition (Adelaide 1977), pp. vi, 155.
22 Philip Batty, 'White Redemption Rituals: Reflections on the Repatriation of Aboriginal Secret-Sacred Objects', in Tess Lea et al. (eds.), *Moving Anthropology. Critical Indigenous Studies* (Darwin 2006), pp. 55–63.
23 Layton 1986, p. 94.
24 Shortly before the climbing ban came into force, there was still a mass influx: see BBC News online 25 Oct. 2019: 'Uluru climbing ban: Tourists scale sacred rock for final time'.
25 See https://fusion.org.au/pilgrimage/ (accessed 17 Sept. 2021); cf. Barnes 2011, p. 174.

Chapter 11

1 David Kinsley, *Ecology and Religion. Ecological Spirituality in Cross-Cultural Perspective* (Englewood Cliffs 1995); Whitney Bauman et al. (eds.), *Grounding Religion. A Field Guide to the Study of Religion and Ecology* (London 2011); Willis Jenkins et al. (eds.), *Routledge Handbook of Religion and Ecology* (London 2017).
2 Lynn White, 'The Historical Roots of Our Ecologic Crisis', *Science* 155/3767 (1967): 1203–07; see also Bron Taylor, 'The Greening of Religion Hypothesis (Part One): From Lynn White, Jr and Claims That Religions Can Promote Environmentally Destructive Attitudes and Behaviors to Assertions They Are Becoming Environmentally Friendly', *Journal of Religion, Nature and Culture* 10/3 (2016): 268–305.
3 Francis 2015, quotations pp. 10, 66, 68; for the prehistory, see Olivier Landron, *Le catholicisme vert. Histoire des relations entre l'Église et la nature au XXe siècle* (Paris 2008).
4 Taylor 2010.
5 Andre Gingrich, 'Hierarchical Merging and Horizontal Distinction – A Comparative Perspective on Tibetan Mountain Cults', in *Reflections of the Mountain. Essays on the History and Social Meaning of the Mountain Cult in Tibet and the Himalaya*, ed. by Anne-Marie Blondeau and Ernst Steinkellner (Vienna 1996), pp. 233–62 (with the distinction between monotheistic/nature-devaluing and polytheistic/nature-valuing scripturalism). There is an extensive literature on the general role of writing in historical developments, from Jack Goody's *The Logic of Writing and the Organisation of Society* (Cambridge 1986).
6 Bruno Latour, *Kampf um Gaia. Acht Vorträge über das neue Klimaregime* (Berlin 2017), p. 34 ('Nature and Culture' as Siamese Twins); quite different is Rein-

Notes to Chapter 11

hard Koselleck et al. (eds.), *Geschichtliche Grundbegriffe. Historisches Wörterbuch der politisch-sozialen Sprache in Deutschland*, 8 vols (Stuttgart 1972–1997), vol. 4, pp. 215–44 ('Natur') and vol. 7, pp. 679–774 ('Zivilisation, Kultur'); word frequency queries are also useful, for example at https://books.google.com/ngrams (accessed 1 Nov. 2022); the use of these scholarly terms among the population at large is poorly studied; until the early 20th century, people seem to have understood 'nature' to mean not least 'genitals' and 'sex drive', perhaps mediated by doctors (*Schweizerisches Idiotikon. Wörterbuch der schweizerdeutschen Sprache*, vol. 4 (Frauenfeld 1901), columns 849–850).

7   Krapf 1964, part 2, p. 24 (trans. from German).
8   Hannah Arendt, *The Origins of Totalitarianism* (Cleveland 1958) (first edition 1951), p. 192.
9   Philippe Descola, *Beyond Nature and Culture* (Chicago 2013) (French original 2005).
10 Descola associates European 'naturalism', characterised by the divide of nature and culture, primarily with the scientific revolution of the 17th century, without clarifying its social relevance and religious context; he only marginally addresses the perceptual tradition of Christianity. In contrast, Keith Thomas' classic historical account of the human–environment relationship emphasises the decline of religious anthropocentrism and the rapprochement with nature (Thomas 1983); cf. Jon Mathieu, 'How Great Was the "Great Divide of Nature and Culture" in Europe? Philippe Descola's Argument under Scrutiny', *Histories* **2022**, *2*(4), pp. 542-551; https://doi.org/10.3390/histories2040036.
11 Francis 2015, pp. 86–120.
12 Toni Huber, 'Why Can't Women Climb Pure Crystal Mountain? Remarks on Gender, Ritual and Space in Tibet', in Per Kvaerne (ed.), *Tibetan Studies. Proceedings of the 6th Seminar of the International Association for Tibetan Studies* (Oslo 1994), vol. 1, pp. 350–71; Huber 1999, esp. pp. 120–27.
13 Fumiko Miyazaki, 'Female Pilgrims and Mt. Fuji. Changing Perspectives on the Exclusion of Women', *Monumenta Nipponica* **60**/3 (2005): 339–91, quote p. 349 (original Japanese).
14 European Parliament, digital archive: https://www.europarl.europa.eu/doceo/document/TA-5-2003-0376_EN.html (accessed 15 Oct. 2021).
15 Speake 2018, pp. 233–237; Athos Pilgrimage Office, with information and online application form: http://mountathosinfos.gr/pilgrims-informations (accessed 17 Oct. 2021).
16 Bingenheimer 2017, p. 23.
17 On the concept of pilgrimage, see Dionigi Albera and John Eade (eds.), *New Pathways in Pilgrimage Studies. Global Perspectives* (New York 2017), pp. 5–9; on the emergence of the term 'tourist', see Mathieu 2015, p. 132; on *sight sacralisation*, see Dean MacCannell *The Tourist. A New Theory of the Leisure Class* (Berkeley 1999), pp. 43–48.

Notes to Chapter 11

18 For the ambivalent feelings that the crowds on Mount Fujiyama left in the wake of Reinhold Messner's search for sacred mountains, see Ch. 1 above; at Uluru it can be observed that tourism may have increased the original sacredness (Ch. 10).
19 Verschuuren 2010, the conclusions on pp. 280–91.
20 Verschuuren 2010, pp. xxi–xxii (original Buryatic), pp. 291–96.
21 Yeh 2014, pp. 194–219, here pp. 200–01 (original Tibetan).
22 Yeh 2014, pp. 213–14.
23 Bron Taylor, Gretel Van Wieren and Bernard Zaleha, 'The Greening of Religion Hypothesis (Part Two): Assessing the Data from Lynn White Jr. to Pope Francis', *Journal for the Study of Religion, Nature and Culture* **10**/3 (2016): 306–78.
24 Durkheim paid little attention to mythology and thus to the Aborigines' reference to landscape (see Ch. 10); Weber addressed the 'mastery of nature' and mentioned, for example, the sacred mountains in China as an element of imperial government: see Max Weber, *Gesammelte Aufsätze zur Religionssoziologie* (Tübingen 1920), vol. 1, pp. 308–12, but his focus was on the relationship of religion to economic development.
25 For the classical definitions: P. Byrne, 'Religion: Definition and Explanation,' in *International Encyclopedia of the Social and Behavioural Sciences* (London 2015), pp. 13060–62; for the open use of the term: Martin Southwold, 'Buddhism and the Definition of Religion', *Man* NS **13**/3 (1978): 362–79; Benson Saler, 'Conceptualizing Religion: The Matter of Boundaries', in ibidem, *Understanding Religion: Selected Essays* (Berlin 2009), pp. 172–80 (first 1997); Taylor 2010, pp. 1–3 (in the course of the study, however, he interprets the 'family resemblance' of religion very broadly and, in my view, pays too little attention to the actors' use of language).

INDEX

A

Aboriginal people *see* indigenous peoples of Australia
Acquaderni, Giovanni 78–79, 82
Aegean Sea 70
Africa 2–3, 17, 93, 111, 113, 117; *see also* East Africa
agriculture 14, 69, 94
Alice Springs 98, 100
Alkhanai 117
Alpine Club 33
Alpine Journal 5, 33
Alpine Museum of Switzerland 64
Alpinism 3–4, 32–34, 70–72, 77
  Catholic 77, 79, 81–82
Alps 28, 30, 33, 69, 70–78, 110, 137–138
Amazon 113
America *see* United States
Americas, indigenous peoples of 2, 84, 87–91, 112–113
Andes 4, 17, 33, *see also* South America
Andrian, Ferdinand Freiherr von 35–37
Angaja 41
Aniconism, Protestant 67–69
anthropocentrism 32, 90, 109–110, 114
anthropology 16, 35–36, 84, 100, 104, 113
antiquity, late antiquity 3, 10, 12, 19–21, 32, 55, 67
Aosta Valley 78
Arizona 17
ascetics 13, 19–20, 45, 114–115
Asia 2–3, 17, 20, 24, 35–36, 49, 62, 65, 110–112, 116–117
Assam 12
assimilation 86, 88, 103
Atacama Desert 17
Athos, Holy Mountain 70, 115
Australia 2, 5, 98–105, 116–117

Australian National Travel Association 101–102
Austria 35, 44, 70–72
Ayers, Henry 99
Ayers Rock *see* Uluru

B

Baptists 82
Barcelona 117
Barnes, Jillian 102
Barns, Thomas Alexander 96
Bavaria 72
Beijing 24–25, 50, 59
Bernbaum, Edwin 37–38, 94
Bhutan 46
Bible, Bible interpretation 19, 29, 62, 67–69, 90, 92, 95
biodiversity 57, 117–118
Bishops 69, 72, 79, 81
Bixia Yuanjun 53–55, 57
Black Elk Peak 84, 88, 90–91
Black Hills 84–91, 111–112
block printing 12–13, 54
Book of Nature 30, 82, 110
Borglum, Gutzon 85–86
British Empire 24, 42, 96, 101
Brown, Peter 19
Buddha, Buddhism 3, 12–16, 20–21, 28, 34–35, 41–49, 61, 65–66, 76, 90
Buddhism, criticism of 47–48
Burke, Peter 12
Burma 36
Bussard, Patrick 75

C

Calvinism 90
canonisation 11–12, 93
Carthusian Order 19

Index

cartography 28, 60
Catholic alpinism *see* Alpinism, Catholic
Catholic Church 9–12, 68–71, 75–83, 84, 91
Cervini, Marcello 10
Chagga 92–94
Changbaishan *see* Paektusan
Cheyenne (indigenous people) 90–91
Chimborazo 32–33, 35, 131
China 16, 20, 24–28, 34–36, 51–55, 58–62, 65, 112, 119
  People's Republic of 42, 50–51, 56–57, 114
Chinese
  Emperors 3, 26, 28, 50–52, 59–61
  scholars/literati 61, 65, 115
Choe Nam-seon 61–62
Christ the Redeemer 67, 72, 77–83; *see also* Jesus Christ
Christianity 2–4, 10–12, 17–22, 29–33, 36–38, 55, 58–83, 88–92, 105, 109–115
Christians, evangelical 62
churches 68–69, 75
circumambulation *see* mountain, circumambulation
civilisation, criticism of 89–90, 113; *see also* industrialisation
civil religion 85, 112
climate protection 116–118
Club Alpino Italiano 77
colonialism 3, 24, 63, 98, 112–114, 120; *see also* imperialism
Communism 42, 50, 56, 58, 62–63
Confucianism 28, 53–55, 61, 112
Confucius 53, 65
Congo 96
Congregation of Rites, Roman 79, 91
Coolidge, Calvin 86
Council of Trent 9–11, 36, 68
Counterculture, American 47
Crazy Horse 86–87
creation 29, 35, 109–110
cross, Christian 67–69; *see also* Summit cross
Cuaz, Marco 77
Cultural Revolution, Chinese 56

D

Dakpa Sheri *see* Pure Crystal Mountain
Dalai Lama 14, 34, 42
Daoism 28
Darchen, monastery 46
Davos 38
decolonisation 113
deification 55, 110; *see also* idolatry
deities *see* Mountain deities
Demchock 46
democracy 85
Descola, Philippe 113–115, 147
desert 5, 17–21, 90, 98, 100, 102, 104–105, 120
Desert Fathers 18–21
Deutscher Alpenverein 49
development policy 2, 5–6, 42, 48, 50, 57, 74
Devil's Tower *see* Mato Tipi-la
dictatorship 58, 112
diversity, cultural 6, 65, 84, 111, 120
Dott, Brian R. 53
Dreamtime 99–102, 104–105
Dschagga *see* Chagga
Dundas, Charles 93
Durkheim, Émile 100, 118

E

East Africa 92–97
ecological
  awareness 57, 75, 109–110
  movement/turn 37–38, 90, 109–110, 116–118
ecology and religion *see* religion and ecology
Ecuador 32, 35
Einsiedeln 11
Eliade, Mircea 36–37, 65
Encyclical letter 81-82, 109–110, 114
Engadine 72, 139
Engelberg 37
environmental
  conference 5, 117
  problems, environmental pollution 76, 109–110, 112–113
  protection 116–118; *see also* nature conservation, reverse environmentalism

Index

Erzberg 70–71
Erzgebirge 30
ethnology *see* anthropology
Europe 3, 9–12, 17–18, 28–32, 35–36, 47–48, 67–83, 85, 92–93, 110–117
Evangelicals *see* Christian, evangelicals
Everest *see* Mount Everest

F

feminism 67
Fischer, Adolf 95–96
Five-Elements philosophy 26
Five Mountains and Ten Temples 20
Five Sacred Mountains 25–28, 35, 50–51, 57, 59, 65
Fort Laramie Treaty 88–89
Four Great Buddhist Peaks 28, 35
Francis, Pope 109–110, 114
Freemasons 78
freethinkers 75
French Revolution 21–23, 72, 119
Fribourg, canton 71, 75
Friedrich, Caspar David 73–74
Fujiyama 18, 56, 114–115
future, future forecast 110, 114, 116, 118–120

G

Gang Rinpoche *see* Kailash
gender roles 114–115; *see also* women
Geneva 68
geography 44, 47, 60, 93
geology 35, 44, 50
geomancy 60
German East Africa 93
Germany 30, 48–49, 56, 93
Gillen, Francis James 100, 144
globalisation 66, 76, 82
God 10, 30, 68, 70, 78, 90, 92, 110
Govinda, Anagarika 44, 47–48
Grande Chartreuse, monastery 19–20
Great Britain *see* British Empire; United Kingdom
Greece 3, 69, 115
greening of religion 37, 109, 118

Grenoble 19–20, 69
Großglockner 71–72

H

Hamburg Geographical Society 95
Harney Peak 84, 91
Harney, William 102
Harrist, Robert E. 652
heathens 29, 32, 42, 92
Hedin, Sven 42–43
height measurement 29–30, 33, 35, 131
Henan, province 25
Heng Shan 25
Héng Shan 25
hermits 13, 19, 45, 61, 70
Himachal Pradesh 1–2
Himalaya 1, 17, 34–35, 42, 44,–46, 57; *see also* Transhimalaya
Hinduism 41–42, 45–48
Hitler, Adolf 44
Hoffmann, Ernst Lothar *see* Govinda, Anagarika
holiness 9–19, 35–38, 45, 67, 82, 88–89, 95, 103–104, 117
Holy
  Mass 77, 81
  Scripture *see* Bible
  Spirit 10–11
  Year 77–80
Hua Shan 25
Huber, Toni 16–17
Humboldt, Alexander von 29, 32–33
hunting, hunting ban 14, 85, 88, 96, 97, 100, 105
Hwanung 61

I

idolatry 4, 32, 62, 68, 82
Iliffe, John 94, 97
imperialism 3, 18, 42, 58, 82, 112; *see also* colonialism
Inca 17
incense 53–55, 65, 118
India 1, 5, 12, 26, 28, 34, 36, 41–49, 76

Index

indigenous
  movement 89–91, 98, 103–105, 113–114, 117–118, 120
  peoples of Australia 98–105
  peoples of the Americas *see* Americas
industrialisation 112, 117, 120; *see also* civilisation
inselbergs 98
International Union for the Conservation of Nature 50, 57, 117
Islam 2, 19, 69, 95, 125
Italy 71, 76–80, 83, 110

J

Japan 18, 20, 26, 36, 56, 58, 61–63, 65, 114
Jesus Christ 10–11, 67–68, 79; *see also* Christ the Redeemer
Johann of Austria, Archduke 72
Joseon Dynasty 60
Judaism 19
judiciary 89, 104
Juval, castle 16–17

K

Kaifang 25
Kailash 2, 16, 38, 41–49, 57, 110–111, 120
Kangxi 28, 51, 59–60
Karlstadt, Andreas 68
Karpo, Pema 12–14
Kathmandu 57
Khawakarbo 118
Kibo 93–94; *see also* Kilimanjaro
Kilimanjaro 92–95, 97, 111, 113
Kilimanjaro National Park 94
Kim Dynasty 62, 112
Kim Il-sung 58, 62–64
Kim Jong-il 58, 63–64
Kleinglockner 71–72
Korea 26, 58, 60; *see also* North Korea, South Korea
Krapf, Johann Ludwig 95
Kullu Valley 1
Kuomingtang 56

L

Lakota Sioux 84–89, 91, 112
Lammer, Eugen Guido 74–75
land rights 89, 103
Latin America *see* South America
Leo XIII, Pope 79, 81–82, 140
Lhasa 14, 42, 46
Li Ping 51
Licancábur 17
literacy, non-literacy 12, 65, 98, 111–112, 146
Little Big Horn 86
Loliondo, Game Controlled Area 97
London 24, 28, 33
Loven, Karl 72
Löwer, Hans-Joachim 75
Luther, Martin 10, 68, 90

M

Maasai 95–97
magic 13, 18, 33, 46, 48, 65, 67, 69, 94
mainstream religion 117
Mallory, George 4
Manasarovar, lake 43, 46–47
Manchu Dynasty 55, 59–60
Manchuria 55, 58–59, 63–64
Mandala 13, 41, 46
Mao Zedong 42, 56
Marconi, Guglielmo 82
Mass *see* Holy Mass
Mato Tipi-la 84, 91
Matterhorn 81
McKay, Alex 45
McMahon Line 12
meditation 13–14, 45
Meiji Revolution 115
Messner, Reinhold 16–19, 38, 97, 127
Milarepa 41, 46
Ming Dynasty 3, 24
Ministry of Rites
  Chinese 55, 112
  Korean 59–60
Miroku, Jikigyo 115
mission, missionaries 75, 84, 88, 92, 94–95, 113, 143
Mombarone 79, 81

Index

monastery 18–20, 25, 61, 69–70, 111; *see also* Darchem, Grande Chartreuse, Nanzen-ji, Rongbuk, St Catherine
Mongolia 61, 133
monks, monasticism 12, 19–20, 28, 41–42, 54, 61, 69–70, 115, 118
monotheism 19, 94, 146
monstrances 11
Mont Blanc 33, 78
Mont Rose 33
Monviso 79
Mount Athos *see* Athos
Mount Everest 4, 28, 34–35, 45, 131
Mount Fuji *see* Fujiyama
Mount Meru (or Sumeru) 46
Mount Rushmore 2, 85–89, 112
Mount Sinai 17–19, 29
mountain, artificial 21–23
mountain ascent
  ban 47, 104–105, 115
  first 16, 33, 72, 93
mountain carving 111
mountain circumambulation 14, 42, 46, 48, 114
mountain deities 1, 52, 60, 95–96; *see also* Bixia Yuanjun, Demchock, Hwanung, Parvati, Shiva, Tai Shan, Tangun
mountain names 64, 69, 85, 91
mountain research 28–32, 44, 72, 77
Mountain States Legal Foundation 91
mountaineering 3, 5, 33–34, 47, 65, 71, 74–75, 77, 86, 93, 97
mountaineering associations 3; *see also* Alpine Club, Club Alpino Italiano, Deutscher Alpenverein
mountains
  general holiness of 5–6, 37–38, 94, 111
  perception of 19–21, 32
Mountford, Charles P. 101, 104
Muir, John 90
museums 16–17, 64, 104
mythology 12, 26, 41, 100, 103, 105

N

Nanzen-ji 20

Nationalism 22, 56, 61, 78, 112
National Parks 38, 89–91, 94, 102, 117
National Socialism 72, 74
naturalists 28–32, 90, 96, 102
nature 10, 36–37; *see also* Book of Nature
  and culture 5, 18, 113–114
  conservation 89, 116; *see also* environmental protection, International Union for Conservation of Nature
  politicisation of 20–21, 119–120
nature reserve 97, 117; *see also* National Parks
nature spirits 94, 97
Nepal 37, 41, 57, 133
Newton, Isaac 28, 30
North Korea 58, 62–64, 112
Novalis 48
nuns 41, 54, 56

O

oaths 9–10, 14
offerings 4, 53–54, 59–60, 84, 90, 96, 118
Ol Doinyo Lengai 95–97, 111
Olympus 3, 33, 42
Ore Mountains *see* Erzgebirge
Orthodox Christianity 19, 69, 115
Otto, Rudolf 36
Ötzi 17

P

Paektusan 2, 58–66, 110, 112
P'an Lei 25–28
Panchen Lama 46
pantheism 90, 139
Paris 21–22, 36, 50, 82
Parvati 41, 46
pastors 30, 33; *see also* priests
patriotism 86, 101
physico-theology 29, 32, 110
physics 30
Pico del Teide 35
Piedmont 79, 81
pilgrimage 4, 13–16, 18, 20, 26–28, 34, 42, 44–56, 61, 79, 102, 112, 114–118
Popes 10, 77–82, 109–110, 114
Pranavananda, Swami 47

Index

prayer 4, 13, 25, 27, 30, 33, 52, 54, 59, 63, 81, 84, 88, 95
priests 9–10, 69–70, 77–78, 81; *see also* Pastors
printing 111; *see also* block printing
progress, progress criticism 48, 56, 62, 72
prostration 46
Protestantism 12, 30, 36, 73, 92, 139; *see also* Reformation
Pure Crystal Mountain 12–15, 110, 114
Pyongyang 62–64

Q

Qing Dynasty 28, 55, 59, 61

R

Ramdohr, Basilius von 73
Rebmann, Johannes 92, 94–95, 113
Red Power Movement 89
Reformation 68–69
relics of Saints 11–12
religion and ecology 109
religion
 concept of 17–19, 33–38, 44–45, 53, 63, 73–76, 88, 94, 100, 109–111, 119
 greening of *see* greening of religion
religious
 freedom 87–89
 studies 4, 29, 35–38, 94
reservations 86, 88–89
Reverse Environmentalism 118
revolutions *see* Cultural Revolution, French Revolution, Meiji Revolution
Rio de Janeiro 5, 82–83, 140–141
rock art 87, 101, 104
rock climbing 90–91
rock inscriptions 51, 112
Rocky Mountains 84
Roman Church *see* Catholic Church
Roman Empire 21, 52
Romanticism 60, 70, 73, 116
Rome 10, 77–79, 81, 91
Rongbuk, monastery 34
Royal Society 28
Russia 42
Ruwa 93, 111

S

sacral/secular, delimitation 5, 69, 100, 118–119
sacralisation 22, 102, 105, 116
sacrament 10–11
sacred *see* Holiness
Sacred Mountains Program 38, 90
sacred natural sites 117
St Catherine, monastery and area 18–19
St Elijah 90
St Francis of Assisi 109
St Michael 69
St Peter's Basilica 80
saints, Christian 11–12, 68–69
Scheuchzer, Johann Jakob 28–29, 32
schools 102
science, scholarship 42–43, 47, 72, 77, 109; *see also* mountain research, naturalists
secularisation 57, 65–66, 116
sexuality 54, 115
shamanism 62, 117
Shandong Province 50
Sheng, Kai 28
Shiva 41, 45–47, 133
Shugendo 65
sins 14, 46, 77
Sioux *see* Lakota Sioux
Six Grandfathers *see* Tunkasila Sakpe Paha
slavery 95
Sonnenspitze 73
South America 5, 17, 32, 117, 142
South Dakota 2, 84–88, 120
South Korea 62
South Tyrol 16
Soviet Union 63–64
Spain 4, 9, 12, 88
Spencer, Baldwin 99–100, 144
spiritual, spirituality 3, 5, 18, 33, 48, 67, 87, 89–91, 103, 113
Standing Bear, Henry 86
state formation 35; *see also* nationalism
Stone Age 98–100
Stubai Alps 72–73
Stutfield, Hugh E. M. 33–34
sublime, sublimity 19, 32, 36, 102

Index

Sulzer, Johann Georg 29–31
summit cross 2, 70–83, 111
Sung Shan 25–28
superstition 28, 47, 55–56, 96, 116
Switzerland 29, 37, 64, 71, 76

T

Tai Shan (mountain) 2–4, 25–27, 50–57, 110, 112
Tai Shan (deity) 52–53
Tang Dynasty 51–52
Tangun 62–64, 112
Tantra, Tantrism 13, 16, 41, 45–46, 114
Tanzania 92, 94, 97
Taylor, Bron 110, 119
television 16, 64, 97
temples 20, 22, 25, 28, 50, 52–57, 63, 70
Ten Commandments 19, 67, 89
theology 4, 36; *see also* physico-theology
Tibet 3, 12–17, 20, 28, 34, 41–49, 57, 76, 110–111, 114, 118, 120
Tibet Initiative Deutschland 48–49
Tibetan Government in exile 42, 48
Ticlla, Maria Poma 4
Tise *see* Kailash
tourism 1, 47, 53, 65, 101–102, 115–117, 120
transcendence 5, 33
Transhimalaya 41, 43
transport revolution 101, 116
transubstantiation 11
Trent 10–12; *see also* Council of Trent
Tsari 12–16, 45–46, 110
Tunkasila Sakpe Paha (Black Hills) 84–87
Tyrol 71–73; *see also* South Tyrol

U

Uluru 98–105, 110–111, 113, 116, 120
Uluru, Paddy 104
UNESCO 19, 38, 50–51, 57, 94, 112

United Kingdom 34, 42, 96; *see also* British Empire
United States 3, 36, 84–85, 89, 94, 103, 109–110, 112, 117
urbanisation 24

V

Vatican 12, 78–79, 82
Vienna 35
volcanoes 17, 29, 58–62, 92–97, 111, 115

W

Wakuasi 95; *see also* Maasai
weapons 95, 100, 103, 113
Weber, Max 118–119
White, Lynn 109
wild game reserve 97
wilderness 75, 90
witches 17, 67, 137
women 53–55, 81, 114–116
World exhibition 78
World Heritage 19, 38, 50, 57, 94, 112; *see also* UNESCO
world religion 19, 117; *see also* mainstream religion
World War, First 44, 74, 93, 96
World War, Second 62, 72, 90, 101

Y

Yangtze, river 54
Yellow River (Huang He) 56
Yunnan 26

Z

Zen Buddhism 20
Zuckerhütl 72
Zugspitze 49
Zurich 28, 68

www.ingramcontent.com/pod-product-compliance
Lightning Source LLC
Chambersburg PA
CBHW041439300426
44114CB00026B/2944